I0815714

GRADUALLY THEN SUDDENLY

STUDY GUIDE

Mark Batterson

GRADUALLY THEN SUDDENLY

STUDY GUIDE

How to Dream Bigger, Decide Better, and Leave a Lasting Legacy

Multnomah
An imprint of the Penguin Random House Christian Publishing Group, a division of
Penguin Random House LLC
1745 Broadway, New York, NY 10019
waterbrookmultnomah.com
penguinrandomhouse.com

Italics in Scripture quotations reflect the author's added emphasis.

A Multnomah Trade Paperback Original

Trade Paperback ISBN 979-8-217-15212-4
Ebook ISBN 979-8-217-15213-1

The Cataloging-in-Publication Data is on file with the Library of Congress.

Printed in the United States of America on acid-free paper

1st Printing

The authorized representative in the EU for product safety and compliance is Penguin Random House Ireland, Morrison Chambers, 32 Nassau Street, Dublin D02 YH68, Ireland.
https://eu-contact.penguin.ie

Bookmaking Team: Editor: Drew Dixon • Production editor: Jessica Choi •
Managing editor: Julia Wallace • Production manager: Richard Elman •
Copy editor: Tracey Moore • Proofreaders: Rachel Kirsch, Carrie Krause

Book design by Simon M. Sullivan

For details on special quantity discounts for bulk purchases, contact
specialmarketscms@penguinrandomhouse.com.

Long vision is daring to dream beyond the dash on your tombstone.

CONTENTS

A NOTE FROM MARK

"How did you become an overnight success?"

Sam Walton, founder of Walmart, answered that rhetorical question in a rather ingenious and inimitable way: "Like most other overnight successes, it was about twenty years in the making."[1]

Any way you slice success, it happens gradually then suddenly. This is the phrase that I borrowed from an Ernest Hemingway novel, *The Sun Also Rises*. When asked how he went bankrupt, one of the characters said,

"Two ways. Gradually and then suddenly."[2]

That's how you go bankrupt, but it's also how you become financially independent. It's how you write a book, run a marathon, fall in love, start a business, and do a thousand other things.

All of us admire people who are successful, yet most of us don't want to make the same sacrifices they made to get there. But you can't have it both ways. It is going to take some blood, sweat, and tears. You must take up your cross and follow Christ. You cannot break the law of sowing and reaping—it will make or break you. There are no shortcuts and no cheat codes. Generally speaking, you *get out* what you *put in*.

Almost anyone can accomplish almost anything if they work at it long enough, hard enough, and smart enough. But it's probably going to take longer than you like, and it will probably be harder than you think. It's going to happen—you guessed it—gradually then suddenly.

I want to help you dream bigger, decide better, and leave a lasting legacy. I want to take a journey with you that is based on the following premise from *Gradually Then Suddenly:*

> Destiny is not a mystery. Destiny is a series of decisions—big decisions and little decisions, predecisions and daily decisions. And every decision has a domino effect. For better or for worse, we look more and more like our decisions every day. The good news? You are one decision away from a totally different life.

We overestimate what we can accomplish in a day or week or month or year, but we underestimate what God can do in a decade or two or three. Play the long game. Long obedience in the same direction is the name of the game. We live in a culture that celebrates the latest and greatest, but God celebrates a lifetime of faithfulness.

Are you ready for a wake-up call? Is it time to find the master key to miracles? Are you looking for the beginning of that breakthrough you stopped believing for?

Let's find out how you can be one decision away from living a totally different life!

HOW TO USE THIS GUIDE

Start each session in this study guide by reading the corresponding chapter in the book *Gradually Then Suddenly*. (Read chapter 1 of the book before engaging session 1 of the study guide, read chapter 2 of the book before engaging session 2 of the study guide, and so on.) As you read, remember to allow yourself—and God—whatever space is necessary to work in your heart and mind.

As you go through each session of the study guide, you'll find four different sections designed to help you develop the long vision, long obedience, and long legacy that lead to breakthrough moments.

1. **Start with Scripture:** Each session begins with a Bible passage that illuminates God's pattern of working gradually then suddenly. This foundation will ground you in biblical truth and help you see how God has always used seasons of preparation to ready His people for breakthrough moments.
2. **Dare to Dream:** Next, you'll explore the power of long vision and God-sized dreams. This section will challenge you to think beyond your current circumstances and embrace the kind of cathedral thinking that builds legacies lasting for

generations. You'll have opportunities to examine your own dreams and consider how God might be growing them.

3. **Make a Decision:** Here you'll focus on the daily choices and disciplines that compound over time into dramatic transformation. This section emphasizes the practical steps of long obedience—the consistent faithfulness that positions you for sudden breakthrough. You'll identify specific decisions you need to make to align with God's pattern of gradually then suddenly.
4. **Live the Story:** Now it's time to apply these principles to your everyday life. Each session includes a featured quote from *Gradually Then Suddenly* that reinforces the session's main theme, followed by reflection questions that help you live out long vision, long obedience, and long legacy in practical ways.

Finally, each session concludes with an inspiring quote from a historical figure or thought leader that reinforces the session's central message and provides additional motivation for your journey.

Importantly, all the material in each session works well for both personal study and group interactions. If you are gathering with a group of people to unpack or discuss each session, be sure to use the prompts and questions included in the **Leader's Guide** at the back of this resource.

GRADUALLY THEN SUDDENLY

STUDY GUIDE

SESSION 1

SIXTEEN MILES UPSTREAM

Based on chapter 1 of GRADUALLY THEN SUDDENLY

START WITH SCRIPTURE

Jesus took the five loaves and two fish, looked up toward heaven, and blessed them. Then, breaking the loaves into pieces, he gave the bread to the disciples, who distributed it to the people. They all ate as much as they wanted, and afterward, the disciples picked up twelve baskets of leftovers. About 5,000 men were fed that day, in addition to all the women and children!

—Matthew 14:19–21, NLT

DARE TO DREAM

Have you ever had a God-sized dream? By definition, God-sized dreams will always be beyond your education, beyond your ability, beyond your resources. You can't do it, but God can. God makes big people by giving them big dreams!

When I was twenty-two, we attempted to start a church on the north shore of Chicago. As that first attempt at church planting failed, it was discouraging and disorienting. But that failure is what opened us up to other options. It's how God got us to make the move from Chicago to DC.

I also learned a valuable lesson along the way: *The cure for the fear of failure is not success, it's failure in small enough doses that you build up an immunity to it.* We discovered that God was there to pick us up, dust us off, and give us a second chance.

Almost every dream I've ever had has gone through death and resurrection. And I might add, detours and delays. The best-laid plans of mice and men fall short of God's good, pleasing, and perfect will. The good news? God's vision for your life is bigger and better than yours. God has blessings for you in categories you can't conceive of.

After that failed church plant attempt in Chicago, we packed all our earthly belongings into a fifteen-foot U-Haul and made the move to DC. We didn't go there to plant another church, but God often has ulterior motives. What seemed like a setback was actually a setup.

On January 14, 1996, nineteen people gathered in a DC public school. We averaged about twenty-five people that first year. Our total income was $2,000 a month, and it cost $1,600 to rent the school where we met. That left $400 for my salary and all other expenses.

The early returns on our church plant were nothing to write home about, but I've learned not to despise the day of small beginnings. Our first Easter, we had forty-three people show up. I was over the moon because we'd never broken thirty, let alone forty. Fast-forward thirty years and we have the joy of hosting the Easter sunrise service at the Lincoln Memorial, where a few more than forty-three show up.

What God-sized dreams have you pursued or thought about pursuing? List a few failures and successes, as well as future dreams.

How did you handle the dreams that failed or faltered? How did you see God's plan and purpose through the process?

Every dream has a genesis story, as does every dreamer.

MAKE A DECISION

You are one decision away from a totally different life.

When I graduated from high school, I got a full-ride scholarship to the University of Chicago. On paper it was the perfect situation. The U of C was one of the top-ranked universities in the country, and I had a starting position on the basketball team going into my sophomore season. That's when I took a prayer walk through a cow pasture in Alexandria, Minnesota, that changed the trajectory of my life.

At the time, I was a PERL major—politics, economics, rhetoric, and law. But I heard the inaudible yet unmistakable voice of

God calling me into ministry. I could have stayed at the University of Chicago and graduated debt-free, but I made the decision to transfer to Central Bible College.

Walking into the admissions office and telling them they could have their full-ride scholarship back was one of the hardest decisions I've ever made. It was also one of the best. If I had stayed at the U of C, I think I would have second-guessed it for the rest of my life. The net result would have been an inaction regret.

That decision doubled as a grand gesture—a defining decision that changed the course of my life.

What are some of the biggest and hardest decisions you have ever had to make? How did these change your life for better or for worse?

Which direction are you moving and why? How have good and bad decisions you've made impacted your future dreams?

LIVE THE STORY

> If you want to bless a city, you have to go sixteen years upstream. . . . For better or for worse, what's happening downstream is always the byproduct of what happened upstream. And that's true in big and small ways.
>
> —MARK BATTERSON, *Gradually Then Suddenly*

Long vision is a vision that is beyond your resources, beyond your ability, beyond your death date. We have a hard time believing God for cities, but God says, "Ask me, and I will make the nations your inheritance."[1] God's vision is always bigger and better than ours!

In the Gospels, there is a story about a little boy who gave his brown-bag lunch to Jesus.[2] In our hands, 5 + 2 = 7. But if you give your five loaves and two fish to God, 5 + 2 = 5,000. In God's hands, it doesn't just add up. It multiplies into a miracle for five thousand people. And there's more left over—twelve baskets—than you started with.

Gradually then suddenly is doing little things like they're big things. And when we do, God has a way of doing big things like they're little things. He can turn your five loaves and two fish into a miracle for five thousand.

I hope this study guide inspires long vision, long obedience, and long legacy. But make no mistake, doubt and discouragement will ding-dong ditch you as long as you live. No one bats a thousand. But just as poorly managed success leads to failure, well-managed failure leads to success.

Success is often two steps forward, one step back. But you can't have a comeback without a setback—without the Crucifixion there is no resurrection. God has a way of turning small steps into giant leaps. How? You should know by now—gradually then suddenly!

What can we learn about Jesus from the story of the loaves and the fishes? Have you ever had a loaves-and-fishes miracle happen in your life?

When you think of the concept of gradually then suddenly, how can you apply that to your life?

What are some specific ways you can begin to think "sixteen miles upstream" this week?

> **Is *all* that we see or seem but a dream within a dream?**
>
> —EDGAR ALLAN POE, "A Dream Within a Dream"

REMINDER

Read chapter 2 of *Gradually Then Suddenly* before engaging in session 2 of this study guide.

SESSION 2

THE LOST WEEKEND

Based on chapter 2 of GRADUALLY THEN SUDDENLY

START WITH SCRIPTURE

Then the LORD said to me,

"Write my answer plainly on tablets,
so that a runner can carry the correct message to others.
This vision is for a future time.
It describes the end, and it will be fulfilled.
If it seems slow in coming, wait patiently,
for it will surely take place.
It will not be delayed."

—Habakkuk 2:2–3, NLT

DARE TO DREAM

When did you last spend time daydreaming? Truth be told, most of us spend far more time doomscrolling! Daydreaming isn't a waste of time. It's one way we steward our God-given imaginations. Maybe that's why God gave us the Sabbath. It's not just a day to rest and recover. It gets us out of our daily routines so we can dream again. If you want to change your perspective, sabbath is great way to change pace and change place.

Do you have a dreaming place? A dreaming time? I get more requests for meetings than I can take, and it's hard saying *no.* But if I took every request, I'd have no margin for dreaming. And that's my job as lead visionary of National Community Church. Tuesdays and Thursdays are meeting days, and they often get scheduled wall to wall. But that buys me Wednesdays and Fridays as dreaming days. That might not work for you, but I encourage you to carve out time in your schedule each week to dream, even if it's just for a few minutes once a week.

Alexander Graham Bell, the inventor of the telephone, had a dreaming place overlooking the Grand River. Thomas Edison had a thinking chair. Carl Jung built his Bollingen Tower for the purposes of meditation. Henry David Thoreau skipped stones on Walden Pond. George Washington Carver took prayer walks through the woods at four o'clock in the morning. And let's not leave out Ernest Hemingway, who inspired the title for *Gradually Then Suddenly.*

"When I am working on a book," said Hemingway, "I write every morning as soon after first light as possible." There is an urban legend that Hemingway would sharpen twenty number 2 pencils before writing. "I don't think I ever owned twenty pencils at one time," said Hemingway. But he had his fair share of writing rituals nonetheless. The first draft of each novel was written on onionskin typewriter paper and laid diagonally across his writing table. He also tracked his daily output on a chart "so as not to kid myself."[1]

At this juncture, I'd better mention that there is a fine line between productivity and creativity. I'm not saying they're inversely proportional, but I'm not saying they're not. Sometimes productivity is the enemy of creativity! Sometimes more is less—it's the law of diminishing returns. You can't put a deadline on creativity! And working seven days a week might actually slow you down. Ideas need to ruminate before they germinate.

If you are going to redeem culture, you can't just criticize it or copy it. You've got to create it. If you are going to reach the next generation with the gospel, you can't just appeal to logic. You've got to capture their imaginations like C. S. Lewis and J.R.R. Tolkien.

When was the last time you deliberately daydreamed? Do you have a place and time for it? If not, where and when can you daydream?

What are some ideas that you've written down? Have you set deadlines to them? How will they get completed?

You are one decision away from a totally different life!

MAKE A DECISION

For more than thirty years, I've kept a journal that is essentially my dreamcatcher. It is the place where I pen my prayers, where I ink

God ideas, and where I count my blessings by keeping track of gratitudes.

"Take captive every thought," said the apostle Paul in 2 Corinthians 10:5, "to make it obedient to Christ." One of the best ways to take thoughts captive is to write them down in a journal of some kind. If you don't write them down, they tend to evaporate!

Do you have a dreamcatcher? Maybe it's time to get one! That's because the best way to personalize, internalize, and materialize goals is to put them on paper. Written goals hold us accountable.

Writing down dreams is one thing, but when do you start to live them out? I think the hardest part of any endeavor is getting to the starting line. Taking that first step is always the hardest, but that's how the journey of a thousand miles begins.

So, do you have something in your mind but haven't started it yet? Maybe it's time to do what I've done. Instead of repeating the old adage of *Ready, set, go,* you should tell yourself, *Go, set, ready.* Yes, you have to plan, but it is too easy to procrastinate. If you wait until you're ready, you'll be waiting for the rest of your life.

Catching dreams takes time but creating them takes trial and error. The first creation always happens in the imagination, but the second creation requires risk. Long vision involves as much perspiration as inspiration. It takes blood, sweat, and tears. And I might add, years!

How do you capture your dreams? What does your ideal dreamcatcher look like?

So, what do you need to start your dream today?

LIVE THE STORY

> There is a moment of conception when a single-cell dream is conceived, but you have to act on the idea in a hurry.
>
> —MARK BATTERSON, *Gradually Then Suddenly*

After telling Habakkuk to write down the vision, the Lord added an exhortation: "The vision awaits an appointed time; it testifies of the end and does not lie. Though it lingers, wait for it, since it will surely come and will not delay."[2] Few things are harder than waiting, especially when you don't have a timeline. Often, the toughest thing to trust is God's timing!

I quoted a popular song in *Gradually Then Suddenly:* "It's gonna take time," sang Beatles legend George Harrison. "It's gonna take patience and time, to do it, to do it, to do it, to do it, to do it, to do it right."[3] It was George Harrison who made that song famous—"Got My Mind Set On You" hit number one on the Billboard charts on January 16, 1988. But he first heard the original on a James Ray album during a trip to the United States in 1963.[4] That was five months before the Beatles' first appearance on *The Ed Sullivan Show*, by the way. How did that song hit number one on the Billboard charts? Two ways—gradually then suddenly!

Life is about the journey and not the destination. I encourage you to enjoy the journey no matter how old you are and no matter what season you're in. Why not start right now? If you do, you'll learn to love gradually as much as suddenly!

Do you have a hard time waiting for things? Do you find it tough to trust God's timing?

What does the expression "Life is a journey, not a destination" mean to you? How can you live out this saying today?

> **It's kind of fun to do the impossible.**
>
> —WALT DISNEY

REMINDER

Read chapter 3 of *Gradually Then Suddenly* before engaging in session 3 of this study guide.

SESSION 3

OPPORTUNITY COST

Based on chapter 3 of GRADUALLY THEN SUDDENLY

START WITH SCRIPTURE

Be very careful, then, how you live—not as unwise but as wise, making the most of every opportunity, because the days are evil. Therefore do not be foolish, but understand what the Lord's will is.

—Ephesians 5:15–17

DARE TO DREAM

In 2004, Blockbuster dominated the home entertainment world. Their only competition was mom-and-pop movie stores. They had sixty thousand employees, nine thousand stores, and annual revenues of $5.9 billion.[1] Two decades later, there is only one Blockbuster store left standing!

In 2000, only 4 percent of homes had a broadband internet connection.[2] If you're old enough to have rented a movie from Blockbuster, you're hearing the sound of that dial-up connection in your head, aren't you? That's probably why Blockbuster turned down the opportunity to buy a DVD-mailing company called Netflix for $50 million in 2004.[3] That price tag might seem steep, but it only represented three and a half days of Blockbuster revenue! Last time I checked, Netflix was worth $515 billion, with a *b*—making it the eighteenth most valuable company in the world.

It's hard to blame Blockbuster. They had no idea that 69 percent of Americans would have broadband internet by 2011.[4] But a little vision would have gone a long way! Long vision isn't just thinking long, it's thinking different. They could have dominated the streaming market, but they got stuck in their old business model. They were focused more on actual costs than on opportunity costs, which is the beginning of the end.

Opportunity costs are hidden costs. They are the loss of potential gain because of indecision or inaction.

Have things come up in your life that you chose not to be a part of? What were the opportunity costs with these decisions?

What is one opportunity currently set before you? What is one step you could take this week toward making the most of this opportunity, as Ephesians 5:16 says?

Opportunity does *not* knock.
You have to knock on it.

MAKE A DECISION

Jeremiah 46:17 is one of the saddest epitaphs in Scripture. It says, "Give Pharaoh, king of Egypt, the name 'Braggart who missed his chance.'"[5]

Let that sink in: Pharaoh would be known as the "Braggart who missed his chance."

Life is an endless series of God-given opportunities—to love, to learn, to serve, to share, to give. Either we're going to have the courage to seize those God-given opportunities, or we'll end up like the man who missed his moment.

Missing a moment will always cause us to ask the question "What if?"

In A.D. 1260, Kublai Khan asked Marco Polo's father to send one hundred Christian missionaries to share the gospel with the Chinese people. His request was never granted. Only two monks were willing to make such a dangerous journey, and they ended up turning back and returning home after becoming fearful of local bandits.[6]

There is a branch of history called counterfactual theory. It asks the what-if questions. What if those one hundred missionaries had made it to China and shared the gospel with the people? How would that have changed the course of China's history? We don't know the answer to that question, but we do know that when we don't go, there are opportunity costs.

In 1905, one missionary was purported to have said, "We have a choice in America. We can give from our abundance and make an investment by sending 1,000 missionaries to Japan, or within fifty years we will be forced to send 200,000 of our boys with guns and bayonets."[7] America sent fewer than a dozen missionaries to Japan, and thirty-six years later, the U.S. sent two million young men to the South Pacific with guns, bayonets, and the atomic bomb.

Of course, there are amazing examples of seizing opportunities as well. Around the turn of the twentieth century, a group of missionaries became known as "one-way" missionaries. When they departed for the mission field, they packed all their belongings into coffins and bought one-way tickets because they knew they'd never return home. A.W. Milne was one of them. He felt called to a tribe of headhunters in the New Hebrides. All the other missionaries to this tribe had been martyred, but Milne found favor. He lived among the tribe for thirty-five years and never returned home. The tribe buried him and wrote the following words on his tombstone: "When he came there was no light. When he left there was no darkness."

Sometimes it's difficult to make a decision, and the decision to *not* go ahead with something leads to regret. Psychologists make a distinction between action regrets and inaction regrets. There are the choices that we wish we hadn't made, but then there are the opportunities we left on the table that left us wondering, *What if?* Inaction regrets ache the soul.

Do you play it too safe?

Do you bury your talent in the ground?

Do you say *no* more often than you say *yes*?

Sometimes the sacrifices we fail to make and the risks we refuse to take are the very regrets that cause us to ache.

Is there a risk you need to take?

What is holding you back from taking that risk?

LIVE THE STORY

> Establishing boundaries is hard to do, but it will save you from a ton of regret. It helps us keep the main thing the main thing.
>
> —MARK BATTERSON, *Gradually Then Suddenly*

"By making us feel worse today, regret helps us do better tomorrow," writes Daniel Pink.[8]

We all have regrets, both about things that were said and done and about things that went unsaid and undone. Either way, we have to learn from those regrets.

Years ago, I found myself stretched so thin in my life that something needed to change. I was leading a growing church and accepting speaking invitations and writing books, all while my wife and I had three young children. At a low point, my wife came and told me, "This isn't what I signed up for." I knew I had some hard choices to make. I needed to reestablish my priority of family first.

I regretted finding myself in that spot where I needed to make some drastic changes in my life. But I realized that if I redeemed those regrets the right way, they could change the trajectory of my life in a positive way.

What are your greatest regrets—action and inaction?

What have you learned from them? And what are you going to do about them?

> **By making us feel worse today, regret helps us do better tomorrow.**
>
> —DANIEL PINK, *The Power of Regret*

REMINDER

Read chapter 4 of *Gradually Then Suddenly* before engaging in session 4 of this study guide.

SESSION 4

CATHEDRAL THINKING

Based on chapter 4 of GRADUALLY THEN SUDDENLY

START WITH SCRIPTURE

I tell you, you are Peter, and on this rock I will build my church, and the gates of hell shall not prevail against it.

—Matthew 16:18, ESV

DARE TO DREAM

One person with uncompromising conviction has the potential to change the course of history. Take, for example, a man named John Chapman, aka Johnny Appleseed.

In 1948, Walt Disney released an animated musical called *Melody Time*. That musical turned a farmer and frontiersman named John Chapman into a folk hero named Johnny Appleseed. The film ends with the narrator saying that clouds are not clouds at all. "They're apple blossoms, if you please, from John's heavenly orchard of apple trees."[1]

Born on September 26, 1774, John Chapman was idiosyncratic to say the least. He walked to the beat of his own drum, and he did so barefoot.[2] I can't imagine what the soles of his feet were like given the fact that he logged an estimated four thousand miles on them. I wouldn't want to be the one to give him a pedicure, that's for sure!

To put that into perspective, the farthest possible distance you can travel in the continental United States—north to south, east to west—is 2,892 miles measured in a straight line from Point Arena, California, to West Quoddy Head, Maine. John Chapman crisscrossed this country one and a half times planting apple seeds.

Johnny Appleseed died of pneumonia on March 18, 1845, at the age of seventy-one. Legend says he planted tens of thousands of trees. But he didn't just plant apple seeds, he also planted mustard seeds. John Chapman was also an itinerant missionary. His theology, like his lifestyle, was unorthodox. But the seeds he planted were orthodox.

Permission to speak frankly? Most people are so busy climbing the ladder of success they fail to realize it's leaning against the wrong wall. "Anything less than a conscious commitment to the important," said Stephen Covey, "is an unconscious commitment to the unimportant."[3]

What do you think about the story of Johnny Appleseed? How did his conviction change the course of history?

What is the Lord looking for in your life? Is the ladder you're climbing leaning on the right or wrong wall?

Long vision is a function of conviction, and the deeper the conviction, the longer the vision.

MAKE A DECISION

Do you want to hear the still small voice of the Spirit? To do that, you have to turn down the volume on all the other voices in your life. One way to do that comes back to a subject we covered in session 2: daydream.

When and where do you dream? Do you have any dreaming rituals?

LeBron James is famous for his pregame ritual of putting chalk on his hands, then throwing a cloud of chalk into the air. It's how he amps himself up. I do the same thing before speaking—no, I don't toss up a cloud of chalk. I always take a knee. It's my way of keeping my ego in check. I pray a simple prayer: "Lord, help me help people."

Before writing, I always take off my shoes. Why? It's holy ground. I don't just type words with a keyboard. I worship God with the twenty-six letters of the English alphabet.

Do you have any sacred rituals?

You do you, but long vision requires a dreaming ritual. My recommendation? If you don't do it early in the morning, it probably won't happen.

> Very early in the morning, while it was still dark, Jesus got up, left the house and went off to a solitary place, where he prayed.[4]

Did you catch the change of pace and change of place? Following Jesus means hacking His habits, and Jesus had a habit of getting up early and getting off the grid. In fact, He once got off the grid for forty days! Jesus loved climbing mountains and walking beaches—go, and do thou likewise!

Praying is a form of dreaming, and dreaming is a form of praying. The more I pray, the bigger I dream. And the bigger I dream, the more I have to pray! It's a virtuous cycle. The net result is long vision.

Jesus did disappearing acts on the regular. Why? Because that's when and where and how He found the margin to dream. Jesus commanded a crowd everywhere He went. There were paparazzi around every corner. So, Jesus would retreat to advance. That's how He kept the main thing the main thing. And He always came back with more clarity of vision. "Let us go on to the neighboring towns so I can preach there as well," Jesus said, "for that is *why* I have come."[5]

I'm not naturally a morning person, but I've disciplined myself to become one. Why? Because 90 percent of my creativity happens before noon. You don't want to read anything I write in the afternoon unless I take a nap. Then I get two windows of creativity. And I might add, Jesus set the standard during a storm on the Sea of Galilee. The fact that Jesus took naps is all the justification I need, but I'll cite one of my favorite studies. A 1995 NASA study found that pilots who took a twenty-six-minute power nap experienced a 54 percent increase in alertness and a 34 percent increase in productivity.[6]

Maybe napping is the key to daydreaming? I recognize that creativity depends on chronotype, but getting a jump on the day will help you jump the curve. If I get up late, I feel like I'm playing catch-up all day! It's in the early morning hours, before the world wakes up, that I tend to get God ideas. Maybe it's time to join the proverbial 5 A.M. club!

Can I offer one more piece of advice? What the eye sees is determined by where the butt sits! The best place to dream is someplace that inspires you. I love praying on top of Ebenezers Coffeehouse and the Capital Turnaround because I have more faith praying on top of a miracle that has already happened.

What percentage of your attitudes and opinions comes from social media and news media? How can you silence those and instead form sacred dreaming rituals?

How can you develop ways to not be conformed to the world around you but instead be transformed by the Spirit of God within you?

LIVE THE STORY

> We don't always think of Jesus in these terms, but there is no greater visionary in the history of humankind.
>
> —MARK BATTERSON, *Gradually Then Suddenly*

The church has taken some hits in recent years because of high-profile failings and fallings. To be honest, many of those wounds are self-inflicted. If you let celebrity culture into the church and put people on pedestals, you're setting yourself up for failure. Only one Person is worthy of worship!

Jesus did not say, "I will build *your* church." And He did not say, "*You* will build My church." He said, "I will build My church"—with an emphasis on *I* and *My*—"and the gates of Hades will not overpower it."[7]

Gates are defensive measures. By definition, the church is called to play offense. We don't take potshots at culture. We invade hell-holes with the light and love of Jesus. C. T. Studd, an English missionary to China, India, and Africa in the late nineteenth and early twentieth centuries, supposedly once said, "Some want to live within the sound of church or chapel bell. I want to run a rescue shop within a yard of hell."[8] The church needs more Studds, and you can quote me on that.

A church that stays within its four walls isn't a church. The church belongs in the middle of the marketplace. We should be known more for what we're *for* than for what we're *against.* We're not just believing for revival in the church. We're also believing for renaissance in culture. We are tasked with the redemption of all things!

I know church hurt is real. News flash: There are no perfect churches because there are no perfect people. Spiritual families can be as dysfunctional as biological families. But the church is still the body of Christ and the bride of Christ. The church is still the hope of the world. No government in the history of humankind, no organization on earth—no NGO or 501(c)(3) nonprofit, no foundation or charitable trust—has done as much collective good as the church, and there is no close second. And many of the organizations that have made a positive contribution to humankind were started by the church.

It was churches who advocated for education. Prior to the Civil War, 165 out of 182 colleges in the U.S. were *Christian* colleges.[9] The church invented academia. It was churches that started hospitals.

Even today, 18.5 percent of hospitals are religiously affiliated.[10] It was churches that started orphanages. And churches have inspired parachurch organizations like Convoy of Hope, World Vision, and International Justice Mission to alleviate poverty and fight slavery.

But our tactic isn't taking potshots at what's wrong. We criticize by creating.

The greatest message deserves the greatest marketing, but that doesn't mean watering down the gospel. Irrelevance is irreverence, but that doesn't mean dumbing down the gospel.

"The church has its greatest relevance to the world," said professor and author Timothy Gombis, "when it is most unlike the world in its corrupted forms."[11] The church offers a counternarrative that is countercultural. "The world needs the church, not to help the world run more smoothly or to make the world a better and safer place for Christians to live," said Stanley Hauerwas and Will Willimon. "Rather, the world needs the church because, without the church, the world does not know who it is."[12]

The church ought to be the most creative place on the planet. We live in a cultural moment when it's wrong to say something is wrong, and I think that's wrong. I'll say it again for good measure: We should be known more for what we're for than for what we're against. Instead of taking potshots at what's wrong, we make room for good things to run wild.

If you are going to redeem culture, you can't just criticize it or copy it. You've got to create it.

Are you focused on the news of the world or the good news of the gospel? In what creative ways can you share this good news?

How can your long vision match God's vision?

When I am working on a book, I write every morning as soon after first light as possible.

—ERNEST HEMINGWAY, interview in *The Paris Review*

REMINDER

Read chapter 5 of *Gradually Then Suddenly* before engaging in session 5 of this study guide.

Long obedience is the key that unlocks our potential and God's promises. It's the key to miracles, the key to breakthroughs, the key to success.

SESSION 5

THE POWER OF SAME

Based on chapter 5 of GRADUALLY THEN SUDDENLY

START WITH SCRIPTURE

My soul is in deep anguish.
How long, LORD, how long?

—Psalm 6:3

DARE TO DREAM

Everybody needs somebody who believes in them more than they believe in themselves. One of those people in my life is Dr. Bob Rhoden. He gave us the green light, despite a failed church plant on my résumé, to give it another go with National Community Church.

When we purchased the crackhouse that we turned into Ebenezers Coffeehouse, it was Doc Rhoden who gave the lead gift of $25,000. You don't forget moments like that or people like that. They leave a permanent imprint on your soul. It was Doc Rhoden who invited me to join him in serving as a trustee for a charitable foundation. What a joy, over the last twenty years, to give millions of dollars in grants to upstart ministries.

Doc Rhoden always has a white-hot word from the Word of

God. I still remember a devotional he shared many decades ago on Deuteronomy 33:16—"the favor of him who dwelt in the burning bush." I had never noticed that verse until he pointed it out, but I've been praying for that kind of favor ever since!

Not long ago we got together for lunch, and Doc pulled out his Bible. It's well read, well worn. His Bible reminds me of something Charles Spurgeon supposedly said: "A Bible that's falling apart usually belongs to someone who isn't."[1] Doc opened his Bible to the book of Hebrews and showed me one of the underlined verses:

> Solid food is for the mature, who by constant use have trained themselves to distinguish good from evil.[2]

Doc Rhoden was captivated by that little phrase *constant use.* There is nothing sexy about it. More like sweaty! It's long obedience in the same direction. It's good old-fashioned grit. It's muscle memory. All that stands between you and your destiny is consistency!

If God puts a dream in your heart, don't take *no* for an answer! Try, try again, for as long as it takes!

Who believed in you before you believed in yourself? Who in your life needs you to believe in them?

What discipline do you need to develop to go to the next level?

____

____

____

____

MAKE A DECISION

In David Blaine's TED Talk, he said that everything he does comes down to one word:

Practice.

"It's practice, it's training and experimenting, while pushing through the pain to be the best that I can be," Blaine stated.[3]

There is an old axiom: *Practice makes perfect.* That's true, but not completely true. If you practice the wrong way, you actually develop bad habits. Perfect practice makes perfect. And it has a name—deliberate practice. I wrote about this in *Win the Day*, so I won't expound on it, but here is a formula for lasting change:

DELIBERATE PRACTICE + DESIRABLE DIFFICULTY = DURABLE LEARNING

It was the Swedish psychologist Anders Ericsson who introduced what would become known as the 10,000-hour rule. To achieve excellence in anything—athletically, musically, academically, and spiritually—requires about ten thousand hours of practice. It also requires near-maximal effort.[4] Desirable difficulty is stressing your body beyond its ability to remain in homeostasis. Anything less than 70 percent effort simply maintains the status quo, which is counterproductive.

If you're doing cardio, near-maximal effort is pretty easy to measure. Your target heart rate is 70 percent of your maximal heart rate. You figure it out by multiplying your age by 70 percent, then subtracting from 208. I'm not sure we can measure near-maximal worship, but anything less than 70 percent effort is going through the motions. And it's a clear and present danger. Once you hear a song thirty times, you no longer think about the lyrics. Maybe that's why the psalmist said, "Sing a new song."[5]

Former Navy SEAL David Goggins is famous for his 40 percent rule. When you think you've given it everything you've got, you've probably only tapped 40 percent of your potential.[6] If you push through that perceived limit, you might just surprise yourself. That's why goals that stretch are so important.

What is something in your life that you're willing to sacrifice and take risks for?

What rituals and habits do you need to make or break to succeed with your goal or dream?

LIVE THE STORY

> Maturity is not a mystery—it's mundanity. It's doing little things like they're big things. It's doing the right things day in and day out. If you do that long enough, sooner or later, you will possess the Promised Land.
>
> —MARK BATTERSON, *Gradually Then Suddenly*

Anyone can fall in love. That happens quickly and easily. Staying in love takes staying power. That's how marriages flourish. That's how jobs become callings. That's how you become the best version of yourself.

Remember Pablo Casals? He loved making music. "Music is the divine way," said Casals, "to tell beautiful, poetic things to the heart."[7] Did Casals have innate talent? No doubt. But he became the best of the best by doing what he loved day in and day out.

If you reverse engineer the success Warren Buffett has achieved as an investor, the secret is the love of learning. The Oracle of Omaha reads five or six hours a day. "That's how knowledge works," said Buffett. "It builds up, like compound interest."[8] That's how he has accumulated $144.5 billion, at last count. But it's less about making money and more about the learning curve. "I just sit in my office," said Buffett, "and read all day."[9]

I'm not sure what goal you're going after or what gift you're trying to grow. But there is only one way you become a Warren Buffett, a Pablo Casals, a David Blaine, or a Doc Rhoden. That one way is actually two ways—gradually then suddenly!

In what areas of your life do you settle for the short game? What parts of your life can you devote to the long game?

Do you find it easy or difficult to believe in the power of same? How can you continue to strive for the power of long obedience in the same direction?

> **Success is stumbling from failure to failure with no loss of enthusiasm.**
>
> —WINSTON CHURCHILL[10]

REMINDER

Read chapter 6 of *Gradually Then Suddenly* before engaging in session 6 of this study guide.

SESSION 6

DARE TO BE DIFFERENT

Based on chapter 6 of GRADUALLY THEN SUDDENLY

START WITH SCRIPTURE

The LORD replied, "I will personally go with you, Moses, and I will give you rest—everything will be fine for you."

Then Moses said, "If you don't personally go with us, don't make us leave this place. How will anyone know that you look favorably on me—on me and on your people—if you don't go with us? For your presence among us sets your people and me apart from all other people on the earth."

—Exodus 33:14–16, NLT

DARE TO DREAM

On a foggy night in 1902, a twenty-six-year-old engineer named Willis Carrier was standing on a train platform when he had a eureka moment. He wondered whether fog could be harnessed to cool buildings.[1] He patented the idea and began selling commercial air-conditioning systems in 1907, and pitched his "Igloo of Tomorrow" at the New York World's Fair in 1939. Eighty years later, Carrier Global is a $66 billion business.[2]

In the realm of innovation, there is a concept called the adjacent possible. That phrase was coined by Stuart Kauffman, and it's a picture of how meta-transformation happens.[3] There is almost always a long chain of causality that makes innovation possible. And the implications and ramifications of each invention have a butterfly effect.

Before the advent of air-conditioning, the population of Florida was fewer than a million people. During the summer months, the heat and humidity were insufferable! So how did Florida become the third most populous state in America? The short answer is air-conditioning.[4] There is no way Walt Disney would have identified the Sunshine State as home to Disney World without it.

Air-conditioning was the adjacent possible that grew Florida's population to twenty-three million people and gave them thirty electoral votes. And those electoral votes have swung more than one presidential election. I don't think Carrier knew his contraption would alter the electoral college, but that is part of the butterfly effect.

"The smartest mind in the world couldn't invent a refrigerator in the middle of the seventeenth century," said Steven Johnson. "It simply wasn't part of the adjacent possible at that moment."[5]

Just as you have to know simple addition before you can do algebra, the adjacent possible is like a stepladder—each step opens new possibilities.

Are there places in your life where you are in a rut? How can you try to do things differently instead of spinning your wheels in the mud?

When was the last time you took a leap of faith? What big changes did you have to make in your life?

Long vision is about going after God-sized dreams, but it takes long obedience to get there.

MAKE A DECISION

The only ceiling on your intimacy with God and impact on the world is daily spiritual disciplines. But there's a catch. Once the routine becomes routine, you must change the routine. It's called the law of requisite variety. If you go to the gym and work out the same way every single time, that routine loses effectiveness because your muscles adapt. You need to confuse your muscles, which is what trainers do.

Isn't that what Jesus did? He didn't do an orientation with His disciples. More like a disorientation. "You have heard that it was said," Jesus told them. "But I tell you . . ."[6] Theologians call these sayings of Jesus the six antitheses: love your enemies, pray for those who persecute you, bless those who curse you, turn the other cheek, go the extra mile, and give the shirt off your back.

I love the maxim "Effort counts twice."[7] Consistency beats intensity seven days a week and twice on Sunday. But sometimes you have to add a little variety to your consistency. Every year, I download a Bible reading plan and try to read it cover to cover. But I also change translations. Why? The NIV and NLT read a little differently, and the KJV reads a lot differently—the Shakespearean English slows me down. It makes me process what I'm reading a little more carefully and consciously.

If you want God to do something new, you can't keep doing the same old thing!

Do you feel stuck in any routines that need to be changed? How can you switch up these routines so your relationship with God grows?

How much consistency do you have in your daily faith journey? What sort of variety do (or could) you add to this consistency?

LIVE THE STORY

> You don't have to finish it, but I'd challenge you to start it. What? Whatever God is stirring in your spirit. If it's running a marathon, download the training plan. If it's getting a degree, submit the application. If it's writing a book, pen a paragraph. If it's getting counseling, make the call.
>
> Will it happen overnight? You should know by now, it'll happen two ways—gradually then suddenly! But you can't finish what you don't start.
>
> —MARK BATTERSON, *Gradually Then Suddenly*

Nobody ever said long obedience in the same direction was going to be easy. It requires holding on to the promise God has given you. And sometimes that means daring to be different, to change the things you're doing.

Remember the story I told you about Robert and Taylor Madu? They started Social Dallas on Easter Sunday of 2021. That church is impacting thousands of people, but I love the backstory. Before launching that church, Robert felt challenged to up his game. He did a twenty-one-day water-only fast. Why? He felt like the Holy Spirit said, "Your current level of discipline will not sustain the leader I'm calling you to be."[8]

Sometimes instead of upping your game, you have to resist the negativity and the naysayers and focus on the end goal. Consider the story of the twelve spies who checked out the Promised Land for forty days. While ten of them remained negative, Caleb and Joshua stayed true to their core convictions. They focused on the promises of God.

Forget the negativity on social media and the naysayers around you. Instead, prove them wrong! Dare to have a different spirit and a different heart that trusts God.

What are the areas of your life that need to be adjusted? What can you do to change them so you can pursue your God-sized dreams?

Do you struggle with the negativity around you? How can you enter your own Promised Land that God has for you?

Imitation is suicide.

—RALPH WALDO EMERSON, *Self-Reliance*

REMINDER

Read chapter 7 of *Gradually Then Suddenly* before engaging in session 7 of this study guide.

SESSION 7

THE CREATIVE MINORITY

Based on chapter 7 of GRADUALLY THEN SUDDENLY

START WITH SCRIPTURE

> Joshua told the people, "Consecrate yourselves, for tomorrow the LORD will do amazing things among you."
>
> —Joshua 3:5

DARE TO DREAM

What is the good life? That question has been long debated by philosophers and theologians. Their answers are as different as those who espouse their opinions. What does Scripture say about the end game, the end goal?

Seek first the kingdom of God.[1]
Above all else, guard your heart, for everything you do flows from it.[2]
Remember your Creator in the days of your youth.[3]

Pick a verse, any verse. All of those are true, but what is true north? Is the Golden Rule the gold standard? Is the Great Commandment the greatest of them all? Or maybe it's the Great Commission?

What is the good life?

Before answering that question, let me tell you what it's not. The good life is *not* no problems. The only people without problems are six feet under. The good life is *not* good money. In the words of The Notorious B.I.G., "Mo money mo problems."[4] The good life is *not* no pain—no pain, no gain. The good life is *not* more vacation time or early retirement. Remember the parable of the talents? The reward for good work was more work. The good life is *not* fame and fortune.

"Chasing fame is like ashes blown by the wind," said Clint Eastwood. "It neither lights fires nor stays in place."[5]

Way too many people are trying to keep up with the Kardashians! "We buy things we don't need," said Dave Ramsey, "with money we don't have, to impress people we don't like."[6] How's that working for you? I've only met a few people who I thought were possessed by a demon, but I've met lots of people who are possessed by their possessions. They don't own things. Things own them. My advice? Stop accumulating possessions and start accumulating experiences.

What is your definition of the good life? Do you find yourself pursuing more money or things, or do you strive to be a good steward of everything you have?

What God-given areas in your life—your time, talents, and treasures—can you give back to Him?

Why not you? Why not now?

MAKE A DECISION

I grew up in the western suburbs of Chicago during the Michael Jordan era. Can you say, blessed and highly favored? Every game Jordan played felt like a human highlight reel, but March 28, 1990, was extra special. Jordan dropped sixty-nine points on the Cleveland Cavaliers. That same game, a rookie named Stacey King scored one point by making one of two free throws. After the game, King was asked about Jordan's legendary performance. "I'll always remember this," quipped King, "as the night that Michael Jordan and I combined to score 70 points."[7] Stacey King was taking a little more credit than he deserved, but individuals don't win championships in team sports. It takes teamwork to make the dream work.

How did David become king of Israel? It wasn't by picking himself up by his bootstraps, that's for sure. To put it bluntly, one person can't accomplish much by themselves. David did what great leaders do—he surrounded himself with thirty-seven mighty men.[8] This was his band of brothers, and their exploits are the stuff of legends. I've written two books about one of those mighty men, Benaiah, who chased a lion into a pit on a snowy day and killed it. Of course, the other mighty men did equally amazing things.

How did they do what they did? Courage begets courage! Shammah "took his stand" in a field of lentils, refusing to retreat.[9] What inspired him to take that risk? A few verses earlier, Eleazar "stood his ground." He fought the Philistines until his hand froze to his sword.[10] David's mighty men were more than a band of brothers, they were the creative minority that helped David assume the throne of Israel.

Several decades ago, a psychologist named Dan Chambliss did extensive research involving Olympic swimmers. He isolated a variable that he called the mundanity of excellence—the consistent performance of ordinary tasks. Greatness happens gradually then suddenly! But many years after that study, Chambliss made an admission. "I left out the most important thing," he said. "The real way to become a great swimmer is to join a great team."[11]

The culture of a team or church or organization has a reciprocal effect on everybody in that ecosystem. A negative culture brings everyone down, but a rising tide of faith floats all boats. I know I'm biased, but I don't think you can attend National Community Church for more than a few weeks and not dream a little bigger, pray a little harder, think a little longer. Why? We've experienced too many miracles not to believe God for the next one! Miracles are in the air.

Are you a part of a team with your church or at work? How can you become a vital part of a team?

Do you believe that one person can't accomplish much by themselves? Who in your life has helped lift you up? Who can you lift up?

LIVE THE STORY

> *You may not influence a million people, but you might influence one person who influences a million people.* It was Moses who delivered the Israelites out of Egypt, but it was Shiphrah and Puah who delivered the deliverer! They certainly get partial credit for Israel's exodus out of Egypt.
>
> —MARK BATTERSON, *Gradually Then Suddenly*

How can you live a good story? The good life is multifaceted. It's good food, for starters. Where are my foodies? It's good friends. It's good music and good movies. But it's more than those things. The good life begins and ends with a good God. He is a good father who gives good gifts to His children. No good thing will God withhold from those who walk uprightly before Him. He is working all things together for good. His will is good, pleasing, and perfect. His gospel is good news.

The good life is good stewardship. It's making the most of the time, talent, and treasure God has given us. It's loving God heart, soul, mind, and strength. It's living for the applause of nail-scarred hands. It's my utmost for His highest.

Does long obedience come with the promise of a life of leisure? Absolutely not! Sometimes long obedience involves long suffering! It's making sacrifices for the greater good. It's taking up your cross for the cause of Christ. It's consecrating yourself to God—time, talent, treasure. Why? Because it's all from Him and it's all for Him.

What sort of amazing things do you want to do for God? What sort of amazing things has He done for you?

What God-given risks can you take? List a set of future-tense possibilities!

> **There are those who look at things the way they are, and ask why? I dream of things that never were, and ask why not?**
>
> —GEORGE BERNARD SHAW, adapted from *Back to Methuselah*

REMINDER

Read chapter 8 of *Gradually Then Suddenly* before engaging in session 8 of this study guide.

SESSION 8

THE BUTTERFLY EFFECT

Based on chapter 8 of GRADUALLY THEN SUDDENLY

START WITH SCRIPTURE

Another message came to me from the LORD: "Zerubbabel is the one who laid the foundation of this Temple, and he will complete it. Then you will know that the LORD of Heaven's Armies has sent me. Do not despise these small beginnings, for the LORD rejoices to see the work begin, to see the plumb line in Zerubbabel's hand."

—Zechariah 4:8–10, NLT

DARE TO DREAM

What is the "butterfly effect"? Simply put, little things make a big difference over time. What is the key exponent in that equation?

Time.

Think about how technology has evolved over the last two hundred years. We went from telegraphs to telephones, from smoke signals to satellite signals, from horses to horseless carriages called cars. Each of those innovations involved a quantum leap in technology and psychology, and each one enabled the adjacent possible. But if you zoom out and look at the big picture, all of them happened gradually then suddenly!

We had some fun looking at some of the infamously poor prognosticators who claimed that people would never want computers to help run their homes, that flying in airplanes was impossible, and that the internet would never become a thing. But have you found yourself making poor prognoses in your own life?

Maybe this is your moment to step up and step in. Don't let what you cannot do keep you from doing what you can.

What sort of small things in your life have accumulated to make a big difference?

Do you put impossibilities on your dreams? How can you begin to take small steps to doing something unbelievable?

Little things make a big difference over time.

MAKE A DECISION

During the Enlightenment, it was common practice to maintain something called a commonplace book. "Commonplacing" involved transcribing inspirational quotes from one's reading. "Scholars, amateur scientists, aspiring men of letters—just about anyone with intellectual ambition in the seventeenth and eighteenth centuries," wrote Steven Johnson, "was likely to keep a commonplace book."[1] I say, bring it back! And I hope this book provides you with a few additions.

I was thirty-five years old when I wrote my first book, but I had already read three thousand books before starting to write one. Can I let you in on a little secret? If I like a book, I study the endnotes. Why? I want to know the author's original sources. Those endnotes are rabbit trails and rabbit holes. The literary historian Franco Moretti calls it "distant reading."[2] What is that? "Distant reading takes the satellite view of the literary landscape, looking for larger patterns in the history of the stories we tell each other."[3]

I always try to have three or four books in my reading rotation, and one of them is almost always a biography. Biography is as close as you can come to an out-of-body experience. It's not just a window into someone else's life; it's a mirror for my own.

Along with distant reading—a large breadth of books—there are some books that demand in-depth reading. I read A. W. Tozer's library of books religiously. In Moretti's words, "It's a theological exercise—very solemn treatment of very few texts taken very seriously."[4]

When I was in grad school, I read a book about how to read a book. I know, it sounds like the department of redundancy department. But that little book by Mortimer Adler appropriately titled *How to Read a Book* is how I developed a system that allows me to quickly retrieve what I read decades ago.

Level one is underlining.
Level two is an asterisk.
Level three is circling.
Level four is an upper dog-ear.
Level five is a lower dog-ear.

Virtually every story in this book that isn't personal is drawn from a lower dog-ear. Truth be told, there is nothing new under the sun! Whether we know it or not, we're building on ideas borrowed from previous generations.

How often do you read? What prevents you from reading more?

Are there skills like reading that you can add to your life? How difficult is it to read a book instead of scrolling on your phone?

LIVE THE STORY

> "There is always one moment in childhood," said the novelist Graham Greene, "when the door opens and lets the future in."[5] Those defining moments are the days when decades happen. They shape our psyches in subtle yet significant ways. They change the trajectories of our lives like the flap of a butterfly's wing!
>
> —MARK BATTERSON, *Gradually Then Suddenly*

Johann Sebastian Bach was a prolific eighteenth-century composer from Germany who had a lasting influence on Western classical music. He was an eighth-generation musician—song lines were in his bloodline. Bach lost both of his parents by the time he was ten years old, but an older brother taught him to play the organ. At age eighteen, he got his first gig as a church organist. The crown prince of Sweden was so amazed by his music that he gave Bach a diamond ring.[6]

Johann Sebastian Bach had an insane work ethic—a Protestant work ethic. During his sixty-five years of life, Bach composed 1,128 pieces of music.[7] "I was obliged to be industrious," said Bach. "Whoever is equally industrious will succeed equally well."[8]

That may sound like hard work, not long obedience. But Bach was motivated by faith: "All music should have no other end and aim than the glory of God and the soul's refreshment."[9] His music was motivated by God, as evidenced by his inscriptions at the beginning and end of his musical compositions. The letters *JJ* inscribed at the beginning of his musical pieces stood for the Latin phrase *Jesu Juva*—"Jesus, help me." And at the end of each composition, he inscribed *SDG,* which stood for *soli Deo gloria*—"to the glory of God alone."[10] That's not a bad way to bookend whatever it is you do. Why not start the day with *JJ* and end it with *SDG*?

"What you *do* in the present," said N. T. Wright, "by painting, preaching, singing, sewing, praying, teaching, building hospitals, digging wells, campaigning for justice, writing poems, caring for the needy, loving your neighbor as yourself—*will last into God's future.*"[11]

What you do matters now and forever. I can't promise that someone will pick up something you write 167 years from now, but you never know.

How did Johann Sebastian Bach demonstrate the butterfly effect? How did he live a life of long obedience to God?

What are things you can do that will last into God's future? How can you be motivated to do them by faith instead of by necessity?

Books permit us to voyage through time.

—CARL SAGAN, *Cosmos*

REMINDER

Read chapter 9 of *Gradually Then Suddenly* before engaging in session 9 of this study guide.

Legacy is not what you accomplish. Legacy is what others accomplish because of you.

SESSION 9

GOOD ANCESTORS

Based on chapter 9 of GRADUALLY THEN SUDDENLY

START WITH SCRIPTURE

> The kingdom of God is like . . . a mustard seed, which is the smallest of all seeds on earth. Yet when planted, it grows and becomes the largest of all garden plants, with such big branches that the birds can perch in its shade.
>
> —Mark 4:30–32

Legacy is the gift that keeps on giving after we are long gone.

DARE TO DREAM

Sometimes we work so hard for such a long time, yet we have nothing to show for it. You have been going to counseling, but your marriage is still in need of repair. You have been paying off your debt, but it still hovers over you. You have been exercising and dieting but still can't lose any weight. You have been praying for something, but God hasn't answered those prayers.

It might seem as if nothing is happening, but is it possible that God is growing your root system?

There is an old axiom: *Rome wasn't built in a day.* A city that size takes centuries to build, but few of us have that kind of patience or persistence. And I might add, imagination. We tend to build to current specifications rather than future needs. In his book *How Should We Then Live?* Francis Schaeffer made this observation:

> The Romans built little humpbacked bridges over many of the streams of Europe. People and wagons went over these structures safely for centuries, for two millennia. But if people today drove heavily loaded trucks over these bridges, they would break. It is this way with the lives and value systems of individuals and cultures when they have nothing stronger to build on than their own limitedness, their own finiteness.[1]

The Burj Khalifa is the tallest building in the world—163 stories that rise 2,717 feet. Construction required 330,000 cubic meters of concrete and enough reinforced steel rebar to stretch one-quarter of the way around planet Earth. If you time your visit just right, you can watch the sunset twice in the same day! Watch it at ground level, then hop on the elevator to the observation deck, and watch it again.

That superstructure is incredibly impressive, but even more impressive is the foundation. Before building up, engineers sunk 192 concrete pilings 164 feet into the ground. There is an old rule in architecture: *The higher up you want to build, the deeper down you need to dig.* The same goes for character. And by character, I mean long obedience in the same direction.

Great leaders aren't driven by the extrinsic motivation of crowds. In my experience, if you want a stage too badly, it means you're not ready for it. You have to die to self, or your ego will get in the way.

Great leaders do disappearing acts like Jesus. He would often withdraw to solitary places. He did all-nighters praying and fasting on mountaintops. He even got off the grid for forty days before his formal ministry began.

Are you seeking the limelight?

Or are you seeking the shadows?

There was a moment in Elijah's ministry, right after speaking truth to power, that God said, "Leave here, turn eastward, and hide yourself by the Brook of Cherith."[2]

God sustained Elijah by commanding the ravens to feed him. According to the Talmud, God made seven provisions during the six days of creation. What are they? One, He commanded the Red Sea to split apart for Israel. Two, He commanded the sun and moon to stand still for Joshua. Three, He commanded the fish to spit out Jonah. Four, He commanded the fire not to burn Hananiah, Mishael, and Azariah. Five, He commanded the lions not to harm Daniel. Six, He created the ram and commanded it to get caught in the thicket for Abraham. Last but not least, He commanded the Baltimore Ravens to feed Elijah.

Can I connect the dots? There was something about this season in the shadows that fueled Elijah's faith. It was a season of consecration. It was shortly thereafter that amazing miracles started happening. After Elijah met the widow of Zarephath, her jar of flour was not exhausted and her jug of oil did not run dry. Then he raised her son back to life. Then he beat the odds by defeating the 450 prophets of Baal in a do-or-die duel.

Are you seeking the stage?

Or are you seeking God?

Seasons of pruning often precede seasons of growth. God pours out His blessing *after* we've spent enough time in the shadows. I often tell church planters that the first five years don't count—and I say that to encourage, not discourage. It's less about growing whatever you are leading and more about growing *you.* If you're growing as a leader, so will whatever it is that you lead.

Can I share a hard-earned lesson? As a young leader, there were stages I desperately wanted to be on—and that was evidence I wasn't ready for them. If you're frustrated because success is happening more slowly than you'd like, maybe God is still laying your foundation. Maybe God is growing your root system!

Can I share one of my favorite promises? Just as there are seasons of planting, there are seasons of harvesting. If you keep doing the right things, the day will come when you can't keep up with the blessing. There will be a sovereign acceleration.

> "In that day I will restore
>   the fallen tent of David.
> I will repair its gaps, restore its ruins,
>   and rebuild it as in the days of old. . . .
> "Behold, the days are coming,"
>   declares the LORD,
> "when the *plowman* will *overtake* the reaper."[3]

There is a sovereign acceleration. The NLT says, "The grain and grapes will grow faster than they can be harvested." You won't be able to keep up with the blessings. The gap between planting and harvesting will close. Amos is promising a productivity, a prosperity, that is nothing short of sovereign. It's God-ordained. It's God-given. It's supernatural provision. You could even call it a multiplication anointing.

Does it seems like nothing is happening in your life? What might God be growing in your root system?

What drives you? Are you driven by seeking the limelight or the stage? How does God use you in silent and unseen ways?

MAKE A DECISION

Legacy isn't measured in minutes—more like millennia! When you do things twice your size, it doesn't mean you'll reap a harvest overnight. It's gonna take time!

In 1996, National Community Church averaged about twenty-five people on a good Sunday. It was during our infancy as a church that I met with a pastor in Northwest DC and discussed a potential merger. It felt like an opportunity to leapfrog because they had a building and we did not. And not just a building—a building on Embassy Row! But I also knew that this church had eight splits in forty years, which was disconcerting to say the least. I felt a check in my spirit, and we walked away from a $10 million building. The merger felt like a shortcut, but I think it would have short-circuited who we were becoming as a church. So, we walked away from that opportunity, by faith.

When God says *no,* sometimes it means *not yet.* Remember the old axiom *What goes around comes around*? Twenty-nine years after walking away from that merger, the opportunity presented itself once again. By faith, we relieved the remaining debt and acquired that property. But we didn't buy it for us—we have no plans to use it. We simply want to leverage the ministries that currently operate out of that church building. We want to lift up their arms like Aaron and Hur did with Moses. Why? Because it's not about the name over the church door. It's about the name above all names. We want to steward it for nations and generations.

What things in your life feel like they're taking their sweet time? Do you feel you have the patience to keep at it and to do it right over and over again?

What opportunities does the future hold for you? What will it take for you to never compromise your convictions?

LIVE THE STORY

> If you're going to dream big, you have to think long. That's what good ancestors do—they do what they do for the third and fourth generation.
>
> —MARK BATTERSON, *Gradually Then Suddenly*

Maybe you're doing something over and over again but you're missing the mark.

At the 2004 Olympic games in Athens, an American sharpshooter named Matthew Emmons had a commanding lead going into the final shot in the final round of the men's fifty-meter rifle three-position competition. The gold medal was all but his. He took aim, pulled the trigger, hit the bull's-eye, and lost the gold medal. Wait, what? How could he lose if he hit the bull's-eye?

Matthew Emmons aimed at the wrong target, thus hitting the wrong bull's-eye! The technical term is *crossfire.* Imagine training for four years, having a three-point lead going into your final shot, and losing the gold medal because you aimed at the wrong target. Now imagine doing that with your whole life! Lots of people are working really hard to make ends meet, but what's the end goal?

Is your life aimed at the right target?

What legacy are you trying to leave?

What is the good life? The answers are as different as different can be. But it's a question each of us has to ask and answer. I, for one, would rather fail at the right thing than succeed at the wrong thing!

The Matthew Emmons story is a little depressing, but there is a silver lining. A Czech Olympian named Katerina was overcome with so much sympathy for Matthew Emmons that she gave him a four-leaf-clover key chain. A few years later, he gave her a ring!

They got married, and they now have four children. He lost the gold but found love—not a bad trade!

I'm mixing metaphors, but some people are so busy climbing the ladder of success they fail to realize it's leaning against the wrong wall. Lots of people aim at fame or fortune. They default to the unspoken definition of success—whoever has the most toys at the end of the game wins. The problem with that is this: All the toys go back in the box at the end of the game. That begs the question "What is the right target?"

The bull's-eye, in my opinion, is something Jesus said in Matthew 25:23: "Well said, good and faithful servant." Read that last "quote" again if you missed it. That's not actually what Jesus said! Talk is cheap! It doesn't say "well planned" or "well posted" either. Permission to speak frankly? Just because you post something on social media doesn't mean you've done something about it. All too often, it's virtue signaling.

"Only one life, 'twill soon be past," said C. T. Studd. "Only what's done for Christ will last."[4] Potential is God's gift to us. What we do with it is our gift back to God. But the greatest legacy we can leave is helping other people tap their God-given potential. That's long legacy—the gift that keeps on giving.

How big are your dreams? Do you believe that God is even bigger than the biggest dreams you might have?

Do you believe deep down that God is "able to do immeasurably more than all we ask or imagine, according to his power that is at work within us"?[5] How can this truth become more real to you today?

> **There are no *ordinary* people. You have never talked to a mere mortal.**
>
> —C. S. LEWIS, *The Weight of Glory*

REMINDER

Read chapter 10 of *Gradually Then Suddenly* before engaging in session 10 of this study guide.

SESSION 10

THE DAY WHEN DECADES HAPPEN

Based on chapter 10 of GRADUALLY THEN SUDDENLY

START WITH SCRIPTURE

> You are not the one to build it; but your son, your own offspring, will build the house for My Name.
>
> —1 Kings 8:19, BSB

DARE TO DREAM

Have you ever taken a stroll through Central Park? That park is a geographical oxymoron, isn't it? New York City has 318 skyscrapers. The first time you visit, it's easy to imagine what the six-inch Lilliputians felt like when Gulliver washed up on the shores of Lilliput. It's hard not to feel small in New York City, unless you find yourself in Central Park. It feels very different, doesn't it?

You probably know this intuitively, but studies have found that the pace of life in big cities is much faster than in small towns. How much faster? According to a Princeton University study, 2.8 feet per second faster![1] And that study was fifty years ago! I have no doubt, the pace has picked up even more. Normal walking speed is 4.6 feet per second.[2] Add 2.8 feet per second to that average baseline, and the net result is 7.4 feet per second, which is a decent marathon pace. At that pace, you'd cover 26.2 miles in five hours and twelve minutes. That's what it's like walking the sidewalks of New York City.

Playing the long game is all about pacing yourself. Just as elite athletes take rest and recovery seriously, spiritual maturity understands the importance of pacing. You can't sprint a marathon. All right, maybe the world-record-holding Kelvin Kiptum could. But I'm not Kiptum, and neither are you. Sometimes slower is faster! And this is not unrelated—sometimes less is more! The law of diminishing returns is real.

Where were we? Ah yes, New York City. When I get off the train at Penn Station and take the escalator up to Seventh Avenue, I swear my blood pressure goes up. But the second I cross 59th Street and enter Central Park, it goes down. That 843-acre park is the most visited park in the country!

Remember the axiom we explored in part 1: *Everything is created twice*? It's so important that I want to double back. It's not just the key to long vision; it's the key to long legacy. How did Central Park become Central Park? The answer is gradually then suddenly.

The Central Park Act of 1853 set aside land "to remain perpetually for the refreshment and recreation of the citizens."[3] The original land acquisition was no easy task. The city had to acquire the titles to 7,250 buildings from 561 owners.[4]

Many years before the passage of the Central Park Act, Frederick Law Olmsted set sail from Staten Island for a tour of the Old World that would last many months. The father of landscape architecture, Olmsted approached his travels like the twelve spies who did reconnaissance in the Promised Land.

Upon landing in Birkenhead, England, Olmsted paid a visit to the local bakery. When learning of the intent of his travel, the baker insisted that they visit the city's "New Park." It was love at first sight. "Five minutes of admiration," said Olmsted, "and I was ready to admit that in democratic America there was nothing to be thought of as comparable with this People's Garden."[5]

That was the moment the door opened and let the future in.

That was the day when decades happen.

Frederick Law Olmsted's résumé is unparalleled as a landscape artist. Every time my wife and I walk our dog around the United States Capitol, we are walking through his original designs. It was Olmsted who decided which trees to plant and where the sidewalks would wind. Our physical reality, our lived experience, is an expression of his imagination. The same is true of the National Zoo, the Biltmore Estate, and Niagara Falls State Park. If you've visited any one of those places, you are living his dream. And that goes for the forty-two million people who visit Central Park each year.

Why did he do it? To inspire your imagination. "A great object of all that is done in a park," said Olmsted, "is to influence the mind of men through their imagination."[6]

"Playing the long game is all about pacing yourself." What does this statement mean to you? How can you apply it to your life?

Have you had moments in your life when a door opened for the future to come in? A day when decades happen? One of those life-changing and legacy-impacting days? How can you look for those in your life?

Our actions and inactions, our decisions and indecisions, matter more than we know.

MAKE A DECISION

"Success is never final," said legendary coach John Wooden. "Failure is never fatal."[7]

From 1964 to 1975, Wooden's UCLA Bruins dominated college basketball by winning ten NCAA national championships. They won seven of those championships in a row! Very few championship teams three-peat, but seven-peat is unheard of. Six times John Wooden was named NCAA College Basketball Coach of the Year. What an incredible legacy!

The Wizard of Westwood ranks as one of the most revered coaches in the history of sports, yet those who knew Wooden would argue that his character off the court was even more impressive than his coaching on it.

John Wooden's college coaching career began at Indiana State Teachers College (now Indiana State University). After winning the Indiana Intercollegiate Conference title in 1947, his team received an invitation to compete in the National Association of Intercollegiate Basketball (NAIB) National Tournament. Wooden rejected the invitation because of the NAIB's policy banning Black players from postseason games. One of Wooden's players, Clarence Walker, was African American. If all his players could not compete, none of them would.

John Wooden's refusal to play in the tournament was the catalyst that caused the NAIB to reverse their policy banning Black players. And the next year, Clarence Walker became the first African American to play in a postseason intercollegiate basketball tournament.[8]

I'll let you decide which legacy is more impressive—ten NCAA championships or the one tournament he refused to play in on principle.

Over twenty-nine seasons, John Wooden won 664 games to only 162 losses. His 0.804 winning percentage is one of the highest of all time. After retiring from coaching, John Wooden was asked what he missed most. It wasn't the game. It wasn't the trophies or championships either. I love his two-word answer: "The practices."[9]

What people in your life have had the biggest impact on you? What about their legacy has influenced you?

What people in the world—famous or not—have had legacies that impacted you? How did they help shape or mold your life?

LIVE THE STORY

> Legacy isn't measured by what we accomplish in our lifetimes. Legacy is measured by our coaching tree, our mentoring chain. It's measured by the investments we make in others that are still earning compound interest twenty years later. It's measured by every act of kindness, every word of encouragement.
>
> —MARK BATTERSON, *Gradually Then Suddenly*

What does the word *legacy* mean to you?

Your greatest legacy will probably have nothing to do with what you do in life or the things you accomplish or acquire. Your legacy will have everything to do with the people whose lives you influence.

Think of some of the examples in chapter 10: Amos Alonzo Stagg, the coach who impacted the lives of all his players; Peggy Campolo, the wife of Tony Campolo; Henrietta Mears, who discipled a young Billy Graham through days of doubt. While they might not be as well-known in the world today, their legacies were leaving their fingerprints on people who ministered to millions!

It doesn't matter what you do for a living, but you are a prophet. As Moses said in Numbers 11:29, "I wish that all the LORD's people were prophets and that the LORD would put his Spirit on them!"

For better or worse, your words and actions have a butterfly effect on the people around you.

Who in your life do you impact the most? List them here, and write down the ways you have made a difference in their lives.

What does it mean to be a prophet? How can you be a better prophet for the Lord today?

> **You're going to meet an old man someday down the road—ten, thirty, fifty years from now—waiting there for you. . . .**
> **That old man will be you.**
>
> —RICHARD HALVERSON, "The Old Man"

REMINDER

Read chapter 11 of *Gradually Then Suddenly* before engaging in session 11 of this study guide.

SESSION 11

DREAM FACTORY

Based on chapter 11 of GRADUALLY THEN SUDDENLY

START WITH SCRIPTURE

> After you have suffered for a little while, the God of all grace, who called you to His eternal glory in Christ, will Himself perfect, confirm, strengthen, and establish you.
>
> —1 Peter 5:10, NASB

DARE TO DREAM

Imagination is a wonderful thing. Anytime something is created, it begins as a spark of an idea in someone's head. That's the first creation. But as I've already said, there is the second creation that involves blood, sweat, and years.

Let's talk a little more about Frederick Law Olmsted. When he paid his first visit to what is now Central Park, it was a quagmire. He made the mistake of wearing nice boots, which were ruined by knee-deep patches of mud. He described the swampland as "a very nasty place."[1] But that present-tense reality didn't deter his future-tense vision.

In 1857, Frederick Law Olmsted was installed as architect-in-chief of Central Park. He oversaw the demolition of old buildings, which involved more gunpowder than the Battle of Gettysburg. More than twenty miles of drain tiles were buried three feet beneath grade. A system of paths, for carriages and for walking, was paved, and thirty-four bridges and archways were built. More than ten million cartloads of earth were shifted by horsepower to regrade the park. And a quarter million trees were planted to provide shade.

My point? Everyone who has ever visited the Central Park Zoo, gone ice skating at Wollman Rink, eaten at Tavern on the Green, or visited the Metropolitan Museum of Art—you owe that memory to the imagination of one Frederick Law Olmsted.

Just as we drink from wells we did not dig and eat from fields we did not plant, we play in parks we did not plan. Everything we enjoy has a genealogy. Every time you take a picture, listen to music, or FaceTime on your iPhone, you owe Steve Jobs and dozens of other unknown engineers at Apple a thank-you. The same goes for the rights and freedoms we enjoy! One of the most sacred places in DC is the Tomb of the Unknown Soldier. We owe the unknown soldiers interred there—and every other soldier that fought in America's wars over the years—a profound thank-you. Their legacy is our freedom, and it bears repeating: Freedom is not free!

"On-site every day," said biographer Hugh Howard, "Olmsted was both designer and builder."[2] Of what? His fingerprints were on absolutely everything! "As he watched, the picturesque English-style landscape that originated in his mind came to life."[3]

How did Frederick Law Olmsted envision Central Park, the U.S. Capitol Grounds, the Biltmore mansion's landscape, and dozens of other projects? He painted mental pictures. "In all parts of the park I constantly have before me," said Olmsted to the Central Park board, "a picture [that] I am constantly laboring to realize."[4]

"Imagination is everything," Albert Einstein supposedly said.

"It's the preview to life's coming attractions." I'm not sure what gift God has given us is His greatest. Is it empathy? Is it creativity? But the metacognitive capacity to imagine the future ranks right up there.

Where did Olmsted paint those mental pictures? In his mind's eye. Central Park is part of Olmsted's legacy, but it was a dream within a dream. The genesis was the People's Garden in Birkenhead, England. The progressive revelation called Central Park was a composite picture of every park Olmsted encountered during his years as a travel writer. Photography was in its infancy, so Olmsted took mental pictures. Then he adapted those ideas to his many projects.

Do you consider yourself a dreamer? Why or why not? What are some God-sized dreams you've held in your life? What happened to them?

What are things you can do in your life that will make a difference long after you're gone?

Dreams beget dreams. You never know when or where or how dreams will be conceived.

MAKE A DECISION

In 2014, National Community Church purchased a $29.3 million city block on Capitol Hill that we branded the Capital Turnaround. It sits on the southeast corner of a 4.7-mile prayer circle I prayed in 1996. When we started redeveloping and repurposing that 100,000-square-foot building, we dug 109 micropiles forty feet deep to reinforce the 1891 columns. Why? So we could build on top of the roof deck. If that acre-and-a-half roof deck were land, the asking price would be somewhere north of $25 million. There is very little land left on Capitol Hill, and they aren't making more of it. A $1 million investment to leverage a $25 million roof deck makes perfect sense, but here's the catch: We have no plans to build on top of the building. Then why did we do it? Because the next generation might want to!

If you visit the Capital Turnaround in Washington, DC, there is a backstory behind all the architectural details. The different flooring—wood, cement, brick, and tile—is a tip of the cap to Denver Milk Market, Anaheim Packing House, Armature Works in Tampa, and many other marketplaces across the country. Even the rocking chairs on "Main Street" are a throwback to Cracker Barrel. The streetcar map stenciled on the wall? It's an ode to the building's history.

Built in 1891, the Navy Yard Car Barn served as the last stop on the red line. This is where streetcars were repaired and rerouted—

the turnaround. The name of the building hints at its history, but it's a double entendre. It's where people's lives are turned around now.

Do you think about future generations? What sort of things can you do for those people?

Is there something in your life that you can begin to build or start to reshape to make an impact for the future?

LIVE THE STORY

> There is a word—*futurity*—whose etymology traces back to the third act of *Othello*.[5] The Scottish writer Sir Walter Scott took that word and coined a phrase—"womb of futurity."[6] It's a metaphor for infinite potential. It's a place of endless possibilities. That's what the Dream Center is. That's what the Dream Center does.
>
> —MARK BATTERSON, *Gradually Then Suddenly*

I shared this movie quote in chapter 11: "Sometimes all you need is twenty seconds of insane courage."[7] That quote from *We Bought a Zoo* has become a rule of life for me. Regardless of the dream God has given you, it's going to take twenty seconds of insane courage. But that's how and when and where miracles happen.

Think about twenty seconds. That's about how long it took for David to sling a stone. Or about how long it took for Benaiah to chase a lion into a pit on a snowy day. It only took about twenty seconds of insane courage for Peter to get out of the boat in the middle of the Sea of Galilee. But the results speak for themselves—David defeated Goliath, Benaiah became King David's bodyguard, and Peter walked on water.

How and when and where will your twenty seconds of insane courage happen?

Faith is being obedient to whatever level of revelation we've been given. Sometimes if you wait for more information and you wait until you're ready and you wait for the perfect circumstances, you'll be waiting the rest of your life!

Is there a decision you need to make or a dream you need to live out?

What might your twenty seconds of insane courage look like? What is the first step you need to take?

Courage is not simply *one* of the virtues, but the form of every virtue at the testing point.

—C. S. LEWIS, *The Screwtape Letters*

REMINDER

Read chapter 12 of *Gradually Then Suddenly* before engaging in session 12 of this study guide.

SESSION 12

KEEP CALM AND CARRY ON

Based on chapter 12 of GRADUALLY THEN SUDDENLY

START WITH SCRIPTURE

Restore our fortunes, LORD,
  like streams in the Negev.
Those who sow with tears
  will reap with songs of joy.
Those who go out weeping,
  carrying seed to sow,
will return with songs of joy,
  carrying sheaves with them.

—Psalm 126:4–6

DARE TO DREAM

One of my favorite comics shows a climber on a quest to discover the meaning of life. He climbs to the top of a mountain where he encounters a wise old sage who reveals the answer.

"What is the purpose of life?" the climber asks the sage.

"'The Hokey Pokey,'" the sage says. "That's what it's all about. Now turn yourself around."

That always strikes me as funny. But the truth is, so often we ask ourselves, *What is the purpose of life?* when it seems like there are so many difficulties and uncertainties facing us. Maybe a dream deferred has left you discouraged. Perhaps your family is falling apart and therapy isn't working. Or you're wrestling with anxiety or depression, and your stomach is in knots.

But maybe, just maybe, you're closer to a breakthrough than you know.

Think about the list of all those people in the Bible who thought they couldn't do something.

Moses said he couldn't speak.

Jeremiah assumed he was too young.

Abraham stated he was too old.

Elijah felt like he was no better than his ancestors.

And Gideon believed he was from the wrong side of the tracks.

The truth is, if you're looking for an excuse, you'll always find one!

What do you think about this list of heroes in the Bible who claimed they couldn't? What amazing things did they do for God's kingdom?

Have you ever used the excuse "I can't" in your life? How and when? Write down how you *can* do something starting today.

Live your life in a way that is worth telling stories about.

MAKE A DECISION

Do you recall the story about Ken Jennings that I shared in chapter 12? Ken was a champion of and currently hosts the game show *Jeopardy!* While he was on a family camping trip as a young boy, his sister didn't like the music he was playing, so she told him to turn it down because it would attract mosquitoes. Ken believed his sister, and that false truth remained with him for decades. It was only when Ken was camping with his wife and his younger brother that he learned the truth. He told his wife what his sister had made him believe, only to hear her burst out in laughter.

If you don't identify the lies you've long believed, those false assumptions have the power to rule your life in big ways.

Is there a life lie that has kept you from discovering your true identity in Christ?

Is there an excuse that has kept you from exercising your full authority as a child of God?

LIVE THE STORY

> There will be moments when you're tempted to toss in the towel. There will be moments when it seems like the boat is about to sink. Those are the moments you have to stand up and rebuke the wind and the waves. That is when and where you have to pronounce your faith: "Peace! Be still!"
>
> —MARK BATTERSON, *Gradually Then Suddenly*

We recently had the joy of welcoming our first grandchild into the world. The first time I held him in my arms, I felt like Simeon: "You may now dismiss your servant in peace."[1]

A few days before he was born, Dr. Curt Thompson was speaking at our church, and he said something I'll never forget: "We come into the world looking for someone looking for us." That's a profound insight, but it's even more poignant when you're holding a newborn grandson in your arms.

As I looked into those baby eyes, do you know what I saw? I saw my reflection! In that moment, my life became less about me! And I might add, my life became more meaningful because it was less about me.

The psalmist said, "Keep me as the apple of your eye."[2] That phrase refers to something precious. You are seen, heard, and loved by God. Your name is tattooed on the palm of His hand. He knows the number of hairs on your head, and He collects your tears in His bottle.[3] But wait, there's more! The Hebrew word for "apple"—*ishon*—refers to the pupil. It literally means "the little man of the eye."[4]

When God looks at you, what does He see? He sees Himself—His reflection, His righteousness. Don't forget who you are and whose you are. Remind yourself regularly: You are the apple of God's eye. You are His progeny, His legacy.

We all have different identities—professional, relational, and educational. We self-identify by the places we live and the teams we love. We identify by the schools we attend and titles we have. But our primary identity is child of God.

I don't know what you do for a living, but you are more than a conqueror.[5] I don't know your height or weight, but you are God's workmanship.[6] I don't know what your ethnicity is, but you were made a little lower than the angels and crowned with glory.[7]

Do you believe your name is tattooed on the palm of God's hand? Why or why not? How can you remind yourself daily about this?

What different identities do you have? Is your primary identity as a child of God easy or difficult to believe?

Whether you think you can, or you think you can't—you're right.

—ATTRIBUTED TO HENRY FORD

LEADER'S GUIDE

Use the following pages to lead a group discussion and interaction for each of the sessions in this study. Remember to adapt the number of questions based on the amount of time available for your gathering, and feel free to adapt or change the questions based on the needs of your group members.

SESSION 1: SIXTEEN MILES UPSTREAM

Start: If you could witness any moment in biblical history, which would you choose, and why?

Discuss:

- What did you find most challenging or encouraging about session 1? Why?
- Mark talks about the "cure for the fear of failure." How do you typically respond when you face failure or setbacks?
- What's the difference between a dream and a God-sized dream? How can you tell the difference?
- When have you experienced what seemed like a setback that later turned out to be a setup for something better?
- What are some "small beginnings" in your life that you might be tempted to despise right now?

Study: Ask a volunteer to read Matthew 14:19–21 out loud, then talk through the following questions as a group:

- How does the story of the loaves and fishes illustrate the concept of "gradually then suddenly"?
- What "five loaves and two fish" do you have in your hands that God might want to multiply?

Pray: Heavenly Father, help us see our setbacks as setups and our small beginnings as foundations for something great. Give us the courage to dream God-sized dreams and the faith to take the first step, even when we can't see the whole staircase. Help us trust Your timing and Your process.

In Jesus' name, amen.

SESSION 2: THE LOST WEEKEND

Start: What's your favorite place to go when you need to think or be creative? Why does that place work for you?

Discuss:

- When was the last time you spent intentional time daydreaming? What happened?
- How do you balance productivity with creativity in your life? Which one tends to win?
- Mark mentions the importance of having a "dreamcatcher." How do you currently capture your ideas and dreams?
- What's the difference between "Ready, set, go" and "Go, set, ready"? When might each approach be appropriate?
- What dream or idea do you have that you've been waiting to start? What's holding you back?

Study: Ask a volunteer to read Habakkuk 2:2–3 out loud, then discuss the following questions:

- Why do you think God told Habakkuk to write down the vision? What's the power of putting dreams on paper?
- How do you handle waiting when God's timing seems slow? What helps you trust His timing?

Pray: Lord God, help us to be faithful stewards of our imaginations. Give us the discipline to create space for dreaming and the courage to act on the dreams You place in our hearts. Teach us to trust Your timing, even when the vision seems slow in coming.

In Jesus' name, amen.

SESSION 3: OPPORTUNITY COST

Start: What's a decision you made that seemed small at the time but ended up having a big impact on your life?

Discuss:

- What's the difference between actual costs and opportunity costs? Can you think of an example from your own life?
- The session mentions being "the man who missed his moment." What are some moments you're glad you didn't miss?
- How do you distinguish between action regrets and inaction regrets? Which type affects you more?
- What are some boundaries you've established to help you keep the main thing the main thing?
- Is there a risk you need to take or an opportunity you've been avoiding?

Study: Ask a volunteer to read Ephesians 5:15–17 out loud, then talk through the following questions:

- What does it mean to "make the most of every opportunity"? How do you practically do this?
- How can we discern which opportunities are from God and which are distractions?

Pray: Heavenly Father, give us wisdom to recognize the opportunities You place before us. Help us have the courage to seize God-given opportunities and the discernment to say *no* to distractions. May we live with intention and purpose, making the most of every moment.

In Jesus' name, amen.

SESSION 4: CATHEDRAL THINKING

Start: What's something you've seen built or created that took much longer than you expected? How did that change your perspective?

Discuss:

- How would you explain "cathedral thinking" to someone who's never heard the concept?
- What's the difference between being driven by crowds versus being driven by conviction?
- Mark talks about seeking shadows rather than the spotlight. Why is this important for long-term success?
- What are some practices, disciplines, or routines that help you connect with God and dream big?
- How can the church be more creative in reaching the next generation? How could you?

Study: Ask a volunteer to read Matthew 16:18 out loud, then discuss the following questions:

- What does it mean that Jesus will build His church? How does this take pressure off us?
- How can we be part of God's long-term vision for His kingdom while living faithfully today?

Pray: Lord Jesus, help us think beyond our own lifetimes and build something that will last for generations. Give us the humility to work in the shadows when necessary and the courage to take risks for Your kingdom. May we be faithful builders of Your church.

In Jesus' name, amen.

SESSION 5: THE POWER OF SAME

Start: What's a skill or habit you've developed through consistent practice? How long did it take to see results?

Discuss:

- What person in your life has believed in you more than you believed in yourself?
- What's the difference between regular practice and deliberate practice? How can you apply this to your spiritual life?
- Mark mentions the 40 percent rule—when you think you've given everything, you've only tapped 40 percent of your potential. Where have you experienced this in your life?
- What discipline do you need to develop to go to the next level in your relationship with God?
- How do you stay motivated during long seasons of seemingly little progress?

Study: Ask a volunteer to read Psalm 6:3 out loud, then discuss the following questions:

- How do you relate to the psalmist's cry of "How long, LORD, how long?"
- What does it mean to have "staying power" in your faith journey?

Pray: Heavenly Father, give us the strength to keep going when progress seems slow. Help us value consistency over intensity and trust that You are working even when we can't see it. Develop in us the discipline and perseverance needed for long obedience in the same direction.

In Jesus' name, amen.

SESSION 6: DARE TO BE DIFFERENT

Start: When was the last time you changed a routine that had become ineffective? What motivated the change?

Discuss:

- What does it mean to "confuse your muscles" spiritually? How can you add variety to your faith routines?
- The session talks about the law of requisite variety. Where do you see this principle at work in other areas of life?
- What's the difference between being consistent and being stuck in a rut?
- How do you know when it's time to change your approach versus when it's time to persevere?
- What's one spiritual discipline you could adjust or change to make it more effective? What might that look like?

Study: Ask a volunteer to read Exodus 33:14–16 out loud, then discuss the following questions:

- What made Moses and the Israelites different from other people? How does God's presence set us apart today?
- How can we dare to be different in ways that honor God and advance His kingdom?

Pray: Lord God, help us break free from routines that have become ineffective. Give us the wisdom to know when to persevere and when to adjust our approach. May Your presence be what sets us apart and makes us different from the world around us.

In Jesus' name, amen.

SESSION 7: THE CREATIVE MINORITY

Start: Think of someone you know who makes everyone around them better just by being present. What is it about them?

Discuss:

- What is "the good life" according to our culture? How does this differ from the biblical definition?
- How does being part of a team or community amplify individual potential?
- What are some examples of "creative minorities" throughout history who made a disproportionate impact?
- Who are the "mighty men" in your life—the people who inspire courage and faithfulness?
- How can you be part of lifting others up rather than just focusing on your own success?

Study: Ask a volunteer to read Joshua 3:5 out loud, then discuss the following questions:

- What does it mean to "consecrate yourselves" in preparation for what God wants to do?
- How can we position ourselves and our communities for God to do "amazing things"?

Pray: Heavenly Father, help us surround ourselves with people who inspire us to dream bigger and live more faithfully. Show us how to be part of a creative minority that brings positive change to our world. May we consecrate ourselves for the amazing things You want to do.

In Jesus' name, amen.

SESSION 8: THE BUTTERFLY EFFECT

Start: What's the smallest thing you've seen make the biggest difference over time?

Discuss:

- How have you seen the butterfly effect play out in your own life or in history?
- Mark talks about "distant reading" versus in-depth reading. How do you balance breadth and depth in your learning? In your spiritual life?
- What are some "lower dog-ear" moments from books or experiences that have stuck with you?
- How do you capture and organize the ideas that inspire you?
- What small action could you start today that might have a big impact over time?

Study: Ask a volunteer to read Zechariah 4:8–10 out loud, then discuss the following questions:

- Why shouldn't we despise small beginnings? What's the danger of overlooking small things?
- How does God use small, faithful actions to accomplish His big purposes?

Pray: Lord God, help us see the potential in small beginnings and faithful actions. Give us patience to invest in things that may not show results immediately but will compound over time. May we trust that You can use our small contributions for Your great purposes.

In Jesus' name, amen.

SESSION 9: GOOD ANCESTORS

Start: What's something you learned or inherited from a previous generation that you're grateful for?

Discuss:

- What's the difference between seeking the limelight and seeking God? How can you tell which one you're doing?
- The session talks about building foundations versus building structures. Which phase are you in right now?
- How do you handle seasons when nothing visible seems to be happening in your life?
- What does it mean to be a "good ancestor"? What legacy do you want to leave?
- How can you invest in the third and fourth generation even when you might not see the results?

Study: Ask a volunteer to read Mark 4:30–32 out loud, then discuss the following questions:

- How does the parable of the mustard seed illustrate the concept of gradually then suddenly?
- What "mustard seeds" might God be planting in your life right now?

Pray: Heavenly Father, help us think beyond our own lifetimes and invest in future generations. Give us patience during seasons when You're growing our root systems rather than showing visible fruit. May we be faithful stewards of the legacy You're building through us.

In Jesus' name, amen.

SESSION 10: THE DAY WHEN DECADES HAPPEN

Start: Describe a single day or moment that changed the trajectory of your life. What made it so significant?

Discuss:

- How do you pace yourself for the long game rather than burning out in the short term?
- What's the difference between a legacy of accomplishments and a legacy of influence on people?
- Who are some people whose legacies have impacted your life, even if you never met them?
- What doors might be opening in your life that could "let the future in"?
- How do you prepare for breakthrough moments during ordinary seasons?

Study: Ask a volunteer to read 1 Kings 8:19 out loud, then discuss the following questions:

- How do you think David felt knowing he wouldn't build the temple himself? How can we handle similar disappointments?
- How should we respond to disappointment? How might experiencing disappointment lead to growth?
- What does it mean to invest in something you might not personally see completed?

Pray: Lord God, help us recognize and be ready for the moments when decades happen. Give us the wisdom to invest in things bigger than ourselves and the humility to plant trees whose shade we may never enjoy. Prepare us for the breakthrough moments You have planned.

In Jesus' name, amen.

SESSION 11: DREAM FACTORY

Start: What's something you've helped create or build that outlasted your direct involvement with it?

Discuss:

- How do dreams become reality through "blood, sweat, and years"?
- What's the difference between imagination and action? How do you bridge the gap between the two?
- The session talks about twenty seconds of insane courage. When have you experienced or needed this in your life?
- What are you building now that might serve future generations?
- How can you balance planning with taking bold action steps?

Study: Ask a volunteer to read 1 Peter 5:10 out loud, then discuss the following questions:

- How does suffering prepare us for the good things God wants to do through us?
- What does it mean for God to "perfect, confirm, strengthen, and establish" us?

Pray: Heavenly Father, give us the courage to turn our dreams into reality through faithful action. Help us endure seasons of difficulty knowing they are preparing us for something greater. May we build things that will serve Your kingdom long after we're gone.

In Jesus' name, amen.

SESSION 12: KEEP CALM AND CARRY ON

Start: What's a lie about yourself that you believed for too long? How did you finally break free from it?

Discuss:

- How do you respond when people tell you that you can't do something?
- What's the difference between making excuses and having legitimate limitations?
- The session mentions that you are "the apple of God's eye." How does this truth impact your daily life?
- What are the different identities you carry, and how do they compete with your identity as a child of God?
- How has this study changed your perspective on God's timing and your role in His plans?

Study: Ask a volunteer to read Psalm 126:4–6 out loud, then discuss the following questions:

- What does it mean to "sow with tears" but "reap with songs of joy"?
- How can we maintain hope during the sowing seasons of life?

Pray: Heavenly Father, thank You for everything You've taught us through this study about Your perfect timing and faithful character. Help us live with confidence in our identity as Your children. Give us patience for the gradual seasons and readiness for the sudden breakthroughs. May we always remember that You are working all things together for our good and Your glory.

In Jesus' name, amen.

NOTES

A NOTE FROM MARK

1. Sam Walton, *Made in America,* with John Huey (Bantam Books, 1993), 45.
2. Ernest Hemingway, *The Sun Also Rises* (Simon & Schuster, 2006), 141.

SESSION 1: SIXTEEN MILES UPSTREAM

1. Psalm 2:8.
2. Matthew 14:13–21.

SESSION 2: THE LOST WEEKEND

1. Ernest Hemingway, "The Art of Fiction No. 21," interview by George Plimpton, *Paris Review,* no. 18 (Spring 1958), www .theparisreview.org/interviews/4825/the-art-of-fiction-no-21-ernest -hemingway.
2. Habakkuk 2:3, BSB.
3. George Harrison, vocalist, "Got My Mind Set on You," by Rudy Clark, *Cloud Nine,* Dark Horse Records, 1987.
4. Gary Trust, "Chart Rewind: In 1988, George Harrison 'Got' Another Hot 100 No. 1 for a Solo Beatle," Billboard, January 16, 2023, www

.billboard.com/lists/george-harrison-got-my-mind-set-on-you-chart-rewind-1988/got-my-mind-set-on-you-george-harrison.

SESSION 3: OPPORTUNITY COST

1. Christopher Harress, "The Sad End of Blockbuster Video: The Onetime $5 Billion Company Is Being Liquidated as Competition from Online Giants Netflix and Hulu Prove All Too Much for the Iconic Brand," *International Business Times,* December 5, 2013, www.ibtimes.com/sad-end-blockbuster-video-onetime-5-billion-company-being-liquidated-competition-online-giants.
2. National Telecommunications and Information Administration (NTIA) and Economics and Statistics Administration (ESA), *Exploring the Digital Nation: America's Emerging Online Experience* (U.S. Department of Commerce, June 2013), i, www.ntia.doc.gov/files/ntia/publications/exploring_the_digital_nation_-_americas_emerging_online_experience.pdf.
3. Harress, "Sad End of Blockbuster Video."
4. NTIA and ESA, *Exploring the Digital Nation,* i.
5. NRSVUE.
6. Allison Auth, "Marco Polo, the Immaculate Heart of Mary and a Missionary Spirit," Denver Catholic, updated January 14, 2025, www.denvercatholic.org/marco-polo-the-immaculate-heart-of-mary-and-a-missionary-spirit.
7. Some sources attribute this to J. M. McCaleb, a missionary to Japan.
8. Daniel Pink, *The Power of Regret: How Looking Backward Moves Us Forward* (Riverhead Books, 2022), 39.

SESSION 4: CATHEDRAL THINKING

1. Wikipedia, "Johnny Appleseed (film)," last modified April 30, 2025, https://en.wikipedia.org/wiki/Johnny_Appleseed_(film).
2. Wikipedia, "Johnny Appleseed," last modified July 18, 2025, https://en.wikipedia.org/wiki/Johnny_Appleseed.

3. "Stephen R. Covey > Quotes > Quotable Quote," Goodreads, accessed July 22, 2025, www.goodreads.com/quotes/7138017-anything-less-than-a-conscious-commitment-to-the-important-is.
4. Mark 1:35.
5. Mark 1:38, BSB.
6. Jay Vera Summer, "What Is a NASA Nap: How to Power Nap Like an Astronaut," Sleep Foundation, updated October 27, 2023, www.sleepfoundation.org/sleep-hygiene/nasa-nap.
7. Matthew 16:18, NASB.
8. C. T. Studd, quoted in Alex Bunn, "Heroes and Heretics: CT Studd," *Nucleus* (September 2013), https://archive.cmf.org.uk/resources/publications/content/?context=article&id=26098.
9. Perry L. Glanzer, "What Is a Christian University?: A New Book That Answers This Question," *Christian Scholar's Review,* November 17, 2023, https://christianscholars.com/what-is-a-christian-university-a-new-book-that-answers-this-question/.
10. David Kelly, "Few Consider Religious Affiliation of Their Hospital, Don't Want Religious Restrictions on Healthcare," CU Anschutz Medical Campus News, January 2, 2020, https://news.cuanschutz.edu/news-stories/few-consider-religious-affiliation-of-their-hospital-dont-want-religious-restrictions-on-healthcare.
11. Timothy Gombis, *The Drama of Ephesians: Participating in the Triumph of God* (IVP Academic, 2010), 163.
12. Stanley Hauerwas and William H. Willimon, *Resident Aliens: Life in the Christian Colony,* expanded 25th anniversary ed. (Abingdon, 2014), 94.

SESSION 5: THE POWER OF SAME

1. "Charles Haddon Spurgeon > Quotes > Quotable Quote," Goodreads, accessed July 22, 2025, www.goodreads.com/quotes/397346-a-bible-that-s-falling-apart-usually-belongs-to-someone-who.
2. Hebrews 5:14.
3. David Blaine, "How I Held My Breath for 17 Minutes," TEDMED,

San Diego, California, October 2009, 19:27, www.ted.com/talks/david_blaine_how_i_held_my_breath_for_17_minutes.

4. Steven Kurutz, "Anders Ericsson, Psychologist and 'Expert on Experts,' Dies at 72," *New York Times,* July 1, 2020, www.nytimes.com/2020/07/01/science/anders-ericsson-dead.html.
5. Psalm 33:3, NLT.
6. WordToTheWise, "THE 40 PERCENT RULE—Powerful Motivational Video | David Goggins," YouTube video, July 5, 2019, www.youtube.com/watch?v=ocIWBpT-AGc.
7. Pablo Casals, quoted in "Casals and the Bach Cello Suites," Vialma Classical, accessed July 22, 2025, www.vialma.com/en/articles/72/Casals-and-the-Bach-Cello-Suites.
8. Nicolas Vega, "Warren Buffett Recommends These 5 Books—Now You Can Listen to Them for Free on Spotify," CNBC, November 11, 2023, www.cnbc.com/2023/11/11/5-must-read-books-from-warren-buffet-that-are-now-free-on-spotify.html.
9. Marcel Schwantes, "In a Few Words, Warren Buffett Reminds Us of a Forgotten Habit That Led to His Success," *Inc.,* November 8, 2021, www.inc.com/marcel-schwantes/in-a-few-words-warren-buffett-reminds-us-of-a-forgotten-habit-that-led-to-his-success.html.
10. This quote is often attributed to Winston Churchill, though sometimes also Abraham Lincoln.

SESSION 6: DARE TO BE DIFFERENT

1. "The Launch of Carrier Air-Conditioning Company: 1903–1914," Carrier, accessed July 23, 2025, www.williscarrier.com/weathermakers/1903-1914/.
2. "Carrier Global Net Worth 2018–2025 | CARR," Macrotrends, accessed July 23, 2025, www.macrotrends.net/stocks/charts/CARR/carrier-global/net-worth.
3. Stuart Kauffman, "The 'Adjacent Possible'—and How It Explains Human Innovation," TED Talk, August 28, 2023, YouTube video, www.youtube.com/watch?v=nEtATZePGmg.

4. Steven Johnson, *How We Got to Now: Six Innovations That Made the Modern World* (Riverhead Books, 2015), 80.
5. Johnson, *How We Got to Now,* 64.
6. See Matthew 5:17–48.
7. Angela Duckworth, *Grit: The Power of Passion and Perseverance* (Scribner, 2016), 35, 71.
8. Robert Madu, "Hurts So Good," sermon, Social Dallas, April 28, 2024, video, 10:27–11:20, www.youtube.com/watch?v=pz7KHrey6aM.

SESSION 7: THE CREATIVE MINORITY

1. Matthew 6:33, ESV.
2. Proverbs 4:23.
3. Ecclesiastes 12:1.
4. Wikipedia, "Mo Money Mo Problems," last modified July 16, 2025, https://en.wikipedia.org/wiki/Mo_Money_Mo_Problems.
5. BamaNomad, "American Actor Clint Eastwood, Aged 94, Recently Gave a Moving Speech," Chevy Tri Five Forums, March 8, 2025, www.trifive.com/threads/american-actor-clint-eastwood-aged-94-recently-gave-a-moving-speech.263322.
6. Dave Ramsey (@daveramsey), "We buy things we don't need with money we don't have, to impress people we don't like. Let's quit that," TikTok video, September 9, 2024, www.tiktok.com/@daveramsey/video/7412676615290834222.
7. Stacey King, quoted in Nick Raguz, "When Stacey King Joked About His Contributions on Michael Jordan's Career-High Scoring Night," *Sports Illustrated,* November 11, 2023, www.si.com/nba/bulls/old-school/when-stacey-king-joked-about-his-contributions-on-michael-jordans-career-high-scoring-night.
8. See 2 Samuel 23:8–39; 1 Chronicles 11:10–47.
9. 2 Samuel 23:12.
10. 2 Samuel 23:10.
11. Angela Duckworth, *Grit: The Power of Passion and Perseverance* (Scribner, 2016), 246.

SESSION 8: THE BUTTERFLY EFFECT

1. Steven Johnson, *Where Good Ideas Come From: The Natural History of Innovation* (Riverhead Books, 2010), 84.
2. Franco Moretti, *Distant Reading* (Verso, 2013).
3. Johnson, *Where Good Ideas Come From,* 224.
4. Moretti, *Distant Reading,* 48.
5. Graham Greene, *The Power and the Glory* (Penguin, 2015), 13–14.
6. *Encyclopedia of World Biography,* "Johann Sebastian Bach," accessed July 23, 2025, www.notablebiographies.com/Ba-Be/Bach-Johann-Sebastian.html.
7. "Bach: Compositions, Children, Biography and More Facts About the Great Composer," Classic FM, accessed July 23, 2025, www.classicfm.com/composers/bach/guides/bach-facts/.
8. Johann Sebastian Bach, quoted in "Casals and the Bach Cello Suites," Vialma Classical, accessed July 23, 2025, www.vialma.com/en/articles/72/Casals-and-the-Bach-Cello-Suites.
9. "Johann Sebastian Bach > Quotes > Quotable Quote," Goodreads, accessed July 23, 2025, www.goodreads.com/quotes/333745-all-music-should-have-no-other-end-and-aim-than.
10. "The Life and Faith of Johann Sebastian Bach: 'Soli Deo Gloria' (to the Glory of God Alone)," Christianity.com, updated December 20, 2022, www.christianity.com/wiki/people/j-s-bach-soli-deo-gloria-to-the-glory-of-god-alone-11635057.html.
11. N. T. Wright, *Surprised by Hope: Rethinking Heaven, the Resurrection, and the Mission of the Church* (HarperOne, 2008), 193.

SESSION 9: GOOD ANCESTORS

1. Francis Schaeffer, *How Should We Then Live?: The Rise and Decline of Western Thought and Culture* (Crossway, 2005), 23.
2. 1 Kings 17:3, BSB.
3. Amos 9:11, 13, BSB.
4. C. T. Studd, "Only One Life," Tony Cooke Ministries, accessed

July 24, 2025, https://tonycooke.org/stories-and-illustrations/only-one-life.

5. Ephesians 3:20.

SESSION 10: THE DAY WHEN DECADES HAPPEN

1. Boyce Rensberger, "Pace of City Life Found 2.8 Feet per Second Faster," *New York Times,* February 29, 1976, www.nytimes.com/1976/02/29/archives/pace-of-city-life-found-28-feet-per-second-faster.html.
2. Wikipedia, "Preferred walking speed," last modified May 30, 2025, https://en.wikipedia.org/wiki/Preferred_walking_speed.
3. Hugh Howard, *Architects of an American Landscape: Henry Hobson Richardson, Frederick Law Olmsted, and the Reimagining of America's Public and Private Spaces* (Atlantic Monthly Press, 2022), 23.
4. Howard, *Architects of an American Landscape,* 24.
5. Howard, *Architects of an American Landscape,* 25.
6. Howard, *Architects of an American Landscape,* 38.
7. John Wooden, quoted in Angela Duckworth, *Grit: The Power of Passion and Perseverance* (Scribner, 2016), 264.
8. Will Price, "Desegregating ISU Basketball: The Story of Clarence Walker," MyWabashValley.com, updated February 19, 2023, www.mywabashvalley.com/news/local-news/desegregating-isu-basketball-the-story-of-clarence-walker.
9. Jerry Crowe, "After Loss of His Wife, Family Keeps Wooden Going," *Los Angeles Times,* March 31, 2000, www.latimes.com/archives/la-xpm-2000-mar-31-sp-14584-story.html.

SESSION 11: DREAM FACTORY

1. Hugh Howard, *Architects of an American Landscape: Henry Hobson Richardson, Frederick Law Olmsted, and the Reimagining of America's Public and Private Spaces* (Atlantic Monthly Press, 2022), 39.
2. Howard, *Architects of an American Landscape,* 50.

3. Howard, *Architects of an American Landscape,* 51.
4. Howard, *Architects of an American Landscape,* 55.
5. William Shakespeare, *Othello,* act 3, scene 4, accessed July 24, 2025, https://shakespeare.mit.edu/othello/full.html.
6. *Merrian-Webster Dictionary,* "futurity," accessed July 24, 2025, www.merriam-webster.com/dictionary/futurity.
7. *We Bought a Zoo,* directed by Cameron Crowe (20th Century Fox, 2011).

SESSION 12: KEEP CALM AND CARRY ON

1. Luke 2:29.
2. Psalm 17:8.
3. Isaiah 49:16; Matthew 10:30; and Psalm 56:8, NLT.
4. *Strong's Exhaustive Concordance,* "380. ishon," Bible Hub, accessed July 24, 2025, https://biblehub.com/hebrew/380.htm.
5. Romans 8:37.
6. Ephesians 2:10, ESV.
7. Hebrews 2:7.

ABOUT THE AUTHOR

MARK BATTERSON is the lead visionary of National Community Church in Washington, DC. One church with a network of churches, National owns and operates Ebenezers Coffeehouse, the DC Dream Center, the Culturehouse, and the Capital Turnaround. Mark holds a doctor of ministry degree from Regent University and is the *New York Times* bestselling author of twenty-five books, including *A Million Little Miracles, Win the Day, The Circle Maker,* and *Chase the Lion.* He also authored the children's books *The Best Worst Day Ever* and *God Speaks in Whispers* with his daughter, Summer Batterson Dailey. Mark and his wife, Lora, live on Capitol Hill in Washington, DC.